QUEEN ELIZABETH'S WOODEN TEETH

and Other Historical Fallacies

Be very, very careful what you put into that head,
because you will never, ever get it out.

<small>THOMAS WOLSEY (c.1474–1530)</small>

QUEEN ELIZABETH'S WOODEN TEETH

and Other Historical Fallacies

Andrea Barham

MICHAEL O'MARA BOOKS LIMITED

First published in Great Britain in 2007 by
Michael O'Mara Books Limited
9 Lion Yard, Tremadoc Road
London SW4 7NQ

A CIP catalogue record for this book is available
from the British Library

Papers used by Michael O'Mara Books Limited are natural,
recyclable products made from wood grown in sustainable forests.
The manufacturing processes conform to the environmental
regulations of the country of origin.

ISBN 978-1-84317-239-0

1 3 5 7 9 10 8 6 4 2

www.mombooks.com

Designed and typeset by Martin Bristow

Printed and bound in Great Britain by Clays Ltd,
St Ives plc

Picture Acknowledgements

Getty Images: 69, 71, 149, 151; Mary Evans Picture Library: 79

CONTENTS

FOR ANITA AND KEITH

FOREWORD

IT is said, in a history book I was recently browsing through, that Boadicea rode a scythed chariot. (She didn't.) It is said (in the same publication) that in the Roman Colosseum, Christians were thrown to lions. (They weren't.) On BBC Television's *Junior Mastermind*, small children were informed that Sir Walter Raleigh 'is said' to have brought back the potato and tobacco from the New World. (Raleigh never *went* to North America.)

Such fictions are so entrenched in our collective consciousness that 'it is said' assertions have become part of our history, despite the fact that they never happened. In this book, I strive to reveal the truth behind eighty historical misconceptions and fallacies, in the hope that 'it is said' history will be forever consigned to the rubbish bin. Why repeat inaccuracies? That's what we have politicians for.

ANDREA BARHAM,
June 2007

Chapter 1

ANOMALOUS ANCIENTS

Vikings wore horned helmets

No modern-day, Viking fancy-dress costume would be complete without a horned helmet. Indeed, Norse Valkyrie and Wagner's *Ring* heroine Brünnhilde is invariably portrayed sporting one. Even the cartoon Viking Hägar the Horrible is depicted with horned headgear. However, the popular helmet featuring two prominent horns is a glaring anachronism.

In *The Viking World*, James Graham-Campbell clearly states that Viking helmets 'did not have horns'. Chris Webster explains in *Vikings and their Origins* that although illustrations of Vikings show horned or winged

helmets, 'No examples of such helmets have been found,' adding that 'poorer warriors would have worn a simple conical helmet, or a leather cap.' In *The Vikings*, it is revealed that this common error results partly from 'mistaken dating by early antiquaries of finds from other northern European cultures' and from 'crude depictions of warrior figures . . . dedicated to Odin'. According to Webster, the raven (Odin's bird) was often depicted on top of the helmet with the wings 'forming a circle to the left and right sides'. He suggests that these wings 'can easily be mistaken for horns, especially as the raven's head often cannot be distinguished in profile'.

Pre-Viking Norse horned helmets did exist, however, as A. F. Harding's work *European Societies in the Bronze Age* features a picture of two beautiful bronze examples from Viksø, Zealand, housed in the National Museum in Copenhagen. The narrow, curved horns are twice the length of the helmet. Such helmets were probably reserved for ceremonial purposes. The two in question certainly look as if they would be very tricky to wear on a daily basis. Given that the Bronze Age finished around 1000 BCE and the Viking era began in the ninth century CE, the Vikings would no doubt have regarded the horned helmet as being nearly 2,000 years out of date: hardly the height of fashion.

So, the next time you are called upon to dress up as a Viking, remember that there is no obligation to don any horned headgear. This way, you're much less likely to have problems using public transport.

All gladiators were male

THE female version of gladiator is 'gladiatrix'. The word exists because female gladiators existed; they were generally thrill-seekers from the upper classes. In *Gladiators: 100 BC–AD 200*, Stephen Wisdom reveals that Roman writer Petronius Arbiter mentions a woman of the senatorial [ruling] class 'fighting as a female gladiator'. Gladiatrixes were the exception rather than the rule. In *Life of Domitian*, late-first-century Roman biographer Suetonius describes how Emperor Domitian 'staged . . . gladiatorial shows by torchlight, in which women as well as men took part'.

Roman satirist Juvenal was appalled by the concept of female gladiators. In *Satire VI: The Ways of Women* he asks, 'what modesty . . . can you expect in a woman who wears a helmet, abjures her own sex, and delights in feats of strength?' Writing a century later in *Roman History*, Roman historian Cassio Dio tells of an expensive festival staged by Emperor Nero where women fought 'as gladiators, some willingly and some sore against their will'. Dio, concerned less with the barbarity, commented that 'all who had any sense lamented . . . the huge outlays of money.' Emperor Titus's festival failed to find favour with him either: 'animals, both tame and wild, were slain to the number of nine thousand;

and women (not those of any prominence, however) took part in dispatching them.'

Wisdom reveals that the British Museum houses a marble relief of two female gladiators. One of these is referred to in the inscription by her stage name, Amazonia. He comments that despite people being routinely hacked to bits in the arena, 'public sensibilities were protected from the sight of bare-chested women fighters.' He further explains that some sources described how such women covered their breasts with a wrap-around bandage and later a 'strophium', which was a band of fabric that served as a Roman sports bra.

Women were repeatedly discouraged from taking up gladiatorial fighting. An entry in *Gladiator: Film and History* reveals that a 19 CE edict known as the *Tabula Larinas* stated that 'it should be permitted to no free-born woman younger than the age of twenty . . . to offer . . . herself as a gladiator.' This was not because of the inherent danger of the sport, but because fighting in the arena was not considered a respectable trade for a well-born Roman.

Emperor Septimus Severus ended the practice in the third century. According to Alison Futrell in *The Roman Games*, he discovered that spectators were making 'disrespectful comments about high-born women'. Watching the butchering of animals and criminals in their hundreds was one thing, but speculating on the amorous capabilities of a well-born woman was quite another!

Slaves built the Egyptian pyramids

ONE of the Seven Wonders of the Ancient World, the Egyptian pyramids have fascinated generation after generation. Fifth-century BCE Greek historian Herodotus first suggested that they were built by Egyptian slaves. In *Histories (Book II)* he relates the tale of King Cheops (also known as Khufu), a twenty-sixth-century BCE Egyptian pharaoh who 'compelled everyone without exception to serve as slaves to his own end'. The historian is quick to add that 'anyone who finds such things credible can make of these Egyptian stories what he wishes.' He then continues the story of evil Cheops, who had the Egyptians working 'in gangs of 100,000 men for three months at a

time'. Herodotus also mentions that Cheops was so wicked that when he ran short of cash for his ambitious scheme, he would raise it by prostituting his daughter. However, in *The Egyptians*, Barbara Watterson states that Herodotus's description 'cannot be substantiated'.

In *Everyday Life in Ancient Egypt*, Jon Manchip White reveals that during this time 'slavery in Egypt . . . was a minor and haphazard affair, and slaves were never numerous,' adding that 'they were almost without exception foreign captives.' Free-born Egyptians were 'seldom sold into slavery; and since it was certainly free-born Egyptians who must have built the pyramids, few of them . . . can have been slaves'.

Some five centuries later, first-century Jewish priest and historian Flavius Josephus claimed in *Antiquities of the Jews* that it was Hebrew rather than Egyptian slaves who built the pyramids. 'It happened that the Egyptians . . . became very ill-affected towards the Hebrews, as touched

with envy at their prosperity . . . [and] set them . . . to build pyramids.' He explained that 'four hundred years did they spend under these afflictions.' The dates, however, are somewhat inaccurate: the Great Pyramids at Giza were built between 2575–2465 BCE, while Moses and the Exodus of the Hebrew slaves from Egypt dates to around 1300 BCE.

Spiro Kostof, author of *A History of Architecture*, suggests that 'we should refrain from seeing the pyramids as the repressive fruit of slave labour' since they were built by a 'regular workforce of skilled masons and craftsmen'. Watterson agrees that 'much of the non-skilled labour on the pyramids was undertaken by peasants working during the inundation season, when they could not farm their lands.' Kostof adds that 'additional men were probably levied to transport the blocks between late July and late October, when the Nile flooded and the population was largely idle.' Watterson explains how 'in return for their services they were given rations of food, a welcome addition to the family diet.' It would appear that the construction of the Great Pyramids of Egypt was a job creation scheme devised to keep the people's welfare in mind.

In *The Pyramids*, Miroslav Verner claims that these craftsmen can be 'compared with craftsmen's guilds in the European Middle Ages'. While Kostof adds that 'the satisfaction that ancient communities derived from working on monuments . . . like Stonehenge . . . was real. The Pyramids of Giza were monuments of hope.'

As for 'slave' builders being sealed alive inside tombs to prevent them from passing on the secrets of the tomb's construction, Watterson dates this myth back to an inscription in the tomb of Ineni. The inscription stated that Rameses IX (who reigned 1126–08 BCE) had supervised the construction of the tomb of Thutmose I and verified that it had been constructed with 'no one seeing, no one hearing'. She explains that far from being expendable 'the men who built the royal tombs were skilled and valued craftsmen, who . . . enjoyed a privileged lifestyle.' In fact, while building Medinet Habu – the mortuary temple of Rameses III – the workmen complained about non-delivery of their building supplies, and when their complaints were ignored 'they went on strike', staging what must have been the first sit-in in recorded history.

In the Roman Colosseum, Christians were thrown to lions

IN a children's history book, I recently read how, in the Roman Colosseum, 'on special days, people flocked to see spectator shows at the amphitheatre.' The entry went on to explain how 'Christians, criminals, and slaves were thrown into a ring with lions and were chased, wounded, and killed.' In *The Innocents Abroad*, celebrated American writer Mark Twain makes the same mistake in his 1869 travelogue by stating that 'in addition to the gladiatorial combats and other shows, they sometimes threw members of the hated [Christians] sect into the arena of the Colosseum and turned wild beasts in upon them.' He added: 'It is estimated that 70,000 Christians suffered martyrdom in this place.'

To put things in context, it would have been difficult to sacrifice Christians in the Roman Colosseum at the time of Emperor Nero's Christian persecutions in 64 CE, since the amphitheatre had yet to be constructed. The Colosseum

wasn't opened until 80 CE by Emperor Titus (he of the animal-slaying shows), by which time the Christian persecutions had abated. Indeed, *The Concise Oxford Dictionary of the Christian Church* reveals that although persecutions never completely died out, they were 'sporadic and ineffectual' until the third century.

In *The Greco-Roman World of the New Testament Era*, James S. Jeffers reveals that 'hundreds of Roman Christians, perhaps several thousand, lost their lives in this [Nero's] persecution' but 'none of these persecutions took place in the Colosseum.' Daniel T. Unterbrink confirms in *Judas the Galilean* that 'the Roman Colosseum was not built until 69 CE, five years after the [Christian] persecution.' He explains that Nero staged his executions in 'the Circus Maximus, a prominent square in Rome'.

The most famous Christian martyr said to have been thrown to the lions in the Colosseum is St Ignatius of Antioch. However, the *Catholic Encyclopedia* concedes that 'the evidence that he was martyred in the Colosseum is far

from decisive.' It points out that after an exhaustive examination of the documents in the case, a Father S. J. Delehave concluded that there are 'no historical grounds' for including the Colosseum in 'the category of monuments dearest to Christians'. Furthermore, in *Roman Presences*, it is acknowledged that 'there is no definite evidence that the Colosseum was used for the execution of Christians.'

The *Catholic Encyclopedia* gives us a clue as to when the tradition may have begun. Sixteenth-century Pope Pius V is said to have 'recommended persons desirous of obtaining relics to procure some sand from the arena of the Colosseum', which, the Pope declared, was impregnated with the blood of martyrs. In 1653, antiquarian Fioravante Martinelli's *Roma ex Ethnica Sacra* [Rome from Heathen made Sacred] cited the Colosseum as the place most sacred to Christian martydom. These days, anyone venerating 'holy' dust from the Roman Colosseum should probably bear in mind that there's nothing holy about it: it's just dust.

Emperor Claudius choked to death on a feather

FIRST-CENTURY Roman Emperor Claudius I is a regular on lists of amusing demises. The feather that supposedly caused the sixty-four-year-old Emperor to choke to death in 54 CE was allegedly being used by his doctor to help him vomit after overindulging at a banquet.

Claudius was a glutton. In *The Life of Claudius*, late-first-century chronicler Suetonius describes how, after gorging, the emperor would 'fall asleep, lying upon his back with his mouth open'. There appears to be at least some truth in the feather remedy as, according to Suetonius, whenever Claudius was in this condition, 'a feather was put down his throat to make him throw up the contents of his stomach.' Thank goodness for the advent of indigestion remedies. (Incidentally, the Romans did not have special rooms in which they vomited. The *Oxford English Dictionary* explains that a vomitorium was 'a passage or opening in an ancient amphitheatre or theatre, leading to or from the seats'. It was simply an exit enabling a large audience to be disgorged from the venue in a matter of minutes. The error appears in Richard Eberhart's 1965 work *Selected Poems*, in which he writes 'Good Boy Man! Your innards are put out / From now all space will be your vomitorium.')

Suetonius does not claim the Emperor died from choking, but states that 'most people think that Claudius was poisoned.' In *Apocolocyntosis*, first-century Roman chronicler

Seneca, writing possibly in the very year Claudius died, gives perhaps too graphic an insight into the emperor's demise. He records that Claudius's last words 'came after he'd let off a louder noise from his easiest channel of communication'. Seneca goes on to regale us with those very words '*Va me, puto concacavi me.*' ['Oh my, I think I've shit myself.'] Seneca adds that 'for all I know, he did. He certainly shat on everything else.' It certainly would appear that something untoward was affecting Claudius's digestive processes.

In *The Annals*, late-first-century Roman chronicler Tacitus claims that 'writers of those times transmitted that the poison had been poured into a delectable dish of mushrooms.' However, Tacitus believes Claudius was *saved* from ingesting the poison by the fortuitous 'opening of his bowels [which] seems to have come to his rescue'. The feather then makes a reappearance, since Tacitus then suggests that as the mushrooms were voided from Claudius's system, a poisoned feather was employed as the real murder weapon. He records that Claudius's wife Agrippina 'called upon the complicity . . . of Xenophon, the doctor' who was 'believed to have inserted into the man's throat, as though to aid his efforts at vomiting, a feather smeared with a quick-seizing poison'. Tacitus's rendition of the tale is repeated by modern author Robert Graves, in *Claudius the God: And His Wife Messalina*.

Roman sources may agree that Claudius was poisoned rather than choked – be it by feather or mushroom. However, an entry in *Who's Who in the Classical World* points out that this theory 'has been questioned'. The findings of V. J. Marmion's research team, which appeared in the 2002 paper 'The Death of Claudius' and was published in the *Journal of the Royal Society of Medicine*, revealed that 'all the features [of Claudius's death] are consistent with sudden death from cerebrovascular [blood-vessels supplying the brain] disease.' So it was quite possible that Emperor Claudius died of natural causes and wasn't poisoned at all, which makes all those Roman chroniclers just a big bunch of gossip-mongers.

Chapter 2

COUNTERFEIT KINGS
(PRE-CONQUEST)

King Arthur had a Round Table

In the Great Hall in Winchester Castle, Hampshire hangs an impressive Round Table displayed high on the wall. It has named places for the King and twenty-four knights. The central inscription reads: 'This is the rownde table of kynge Arthur w[ith] xxiiii of hys namyde knyttes.' The names appear round the edge, with those of Galahad and Mordred on either side of the King. It's in remarkably good condition for an allegedly 'sixth-century artefact'. It also has a huge Tudor rose painted in the centre, which helpfully reveals its true origins.

The truth of the matter is that the great King Arthur of Britain who supposedly reigned in the sixth century never existed. In the *Oxford Dictionary of National Biography*, O. J. Padel states that 'Arthur is not mentioned in any contemporary record.' What's more, there is no clear indication how or where the legend arose. 'King' Arthur became known internationally thanks to the twelfth-century work of Geoffrey of Monmouth, *Historia regum Britanniae* [*The History of the Kings of Britain*] (Volume VI), in which the King is described as 'the most renowned Arthur, whose heroic and wonderful actions have justly rendered his name famous to posterity.' King Arthur's Round Table, a marvellous tool to diplomacy where no single knight could claim precedence over another, was also added in the twelfth century. Wace of Jersey's Norman-French version of the tale, *Le Roman de Brut,* has 'rois Artus' install 'la Roonde Table'.

In *A Dictionary of English Folklore*, its editors Simpson and Roud explain that the Winchester Castle table was made in the fourteenth century, possibly for Edward III who, in 1344, planned to found an 'Order of the Round Table'. The *Hutchinson Encyclopedia* suggests that it might be 'the relic of a joust, as the Round Table gave its name, from the twelfth century, to a form of tournament where knights may have played the part of Arthurian characters'. Simpson and Roud add that in 1522, King Henry VIII gave the table a makeover, adding the Tudor rose and a portrait of Arthur modelled on himself, just for good measure.

Sadly, neither the wise King Arthur nor his egalitarian Round Table ever existed, but it still doesn't stop it being a jolly good story, though.

King Alfred burnt the cakes

NINTH-CENTURY King Alfred is the only monarch to be honoured with the title 'The Great', yet he is more famed in popular culture for having burnt some cakes.

In *A Child's History of England*, Charles Dickens explains that 'one fatal winter, in the fourth year of King Alfred's reign,' on the run from the Danes, King Alfred disguised himself as a 'common peasant' and took refuge 'in the cottage of one of his cowherds who did not know his face'. The cowherd's wife left him 'to watch some cakes

which she put to bake upon the hearth'. However, 'being at work upon his bows and arrows . . . his noble mind forgot the cakes, and they were burnt.' The cowherd's wife returned and scolded him saying that he would be 'ready enough to eat them' yet he 'cannot watch them'. She finished by branding him an 'idle dog'. The moral of the story is: *don't leave your monarch in charge of your cookery* . . . perhaps.

It is possible that the story's enduring appeal lies in the fact that many people, were they to admit it, have a sneaking suspicion that nobles, when faced with household practicalities, would be found sadly wanting.

The tale first appeared in 1574, when antiquarian Archbishop Matthew Parker published the *Life of King Alfred,* which was written by Bishop Asser in 893. As the bishop was a friend and counsellor of King Alfred, he was considered a reliable source. However, as is revealed in Lapidge and Keynes's *Alfred the Great,* the tale of the cakes 'does not . . . originate in Asser's *Life of King Alfred*'. According to Robert Gambles in *Breaking Butterflies,* it transpired that Archbishop Parker rashly incorporated 'extensive tracks' from a tenth-century work called *Life of St Neot* into the historically accurate work of Bishop Asser. Parker seems to have been so impressed by the details of the King laying 'in hiding with a certain cowherd . . .' in the *Life of St Neot,* that he felt convinced the tale had to be included in his updated version of Bishop Asser's work.

The anonymous author of *Life of St Neot,* as quoted by Parker, claims that the disguised King stayed at a swineherd's cottage 'content with the bare necessities' while he pondered the wise and godly counsel of his new best friend, St Neot. One day, the swineherd's wife 'entrusted some kneaded flour to the husband of sea-borne Venus'. (Vulcan is the god of fire, so we can surmise that the author is referring to the oven. With such an overblown prose style, no wonder he wished to remain anonymous.) Meanwhile, Mrs Swineherd had been 'intent on other domestic occupations' when she 'saw it

burning from the other side of the room'. She grew angry and said to the King, 'Look here, man, you hesitate to turn the loaves which you see to be burning, yet you're quite happy to eat them when they come warm from the oven!' The King was 'somewhat shaken, and submitting to the woman's scolding' he not only turned the bread, but even 'attended to it as she brought out the loaves when they were ready'. This version has a totally different tone, with King Alfred falling foul of a crotchety woman who was feeling overworked and under-appreciated. It's also much more amusing.

Lapidge and Keynes suggest that the author incorporated the tale into St Neot's biography perhaps because he wanted to 'establish the historicity of St Neot' or possibly because he needed to pad out his story. Little did he know that his fictional anecdote would finish up as the only thing many modern-day people think they know about the great King Alfred. What an unfortunate legacy ...

Ethelred the Unready was so called because he was ill-prepared

THE Danish invasion of England in the late tenth century certainly took King Ethelred II by surprise, but this was not how he acquired his nickname. In *Saxon and Norman Kings*, Christopher Brooke explains that the name Ethelred is a compound of two old English words, *æthel* and *ræd*, meaning 'noble' and 'counsel' [advice]. Simon Keynes's entry in the *Oxford Dictionary of National Biography* explains that although the name was quite a common one of the time, 'contemporaries might well have been more than usually conscious of its literal significance when applied to a king.' In other words, if you're going to be called King 'Well-advised', you had better be a good one.

In 1011, while Ethelred was still on the throne (just), tongues started wagging. In *Breaking Butterflies*, Robert Gambles reveals that an Anglo-Saxon chronicler of the time 'referred . . . to Ethelred as "un-raed", lacking in counsel', though it's not certain exactly what Ethelred's failings were. Brooke explains that 'unræd' could also have meant that 'he did not take the advice they [his followers] gave; or that he had no followers to give advice; or simply that he was unwise' and suggests that 'there would be some truth in all of these statements.'

In March 978, when Ethelred was only ten years old, he became king following the murder of his half-brother, Edward the Martyr. At the time, England was under threat from the marauding Vikings, and whether it was due to youthfulness or inexperience, he did not seem able to work out how best to deal with the threat of invasion. After trying and failing to buy peace with the Danes, he attempted to slaughter them just as they had started to settle. In 1013, Ethelred then sought exile in Normandy and England was ruled briefly by Danish king Sweyn Forkbeard before Ethelred returned a year later upon Forkbeard's death.

The upshot of this idiosyncratic approach to ruling meant that in some quarters Ethelred became a laughing stock, with his detractors employing the rhyming pun 'Ethelred the Unraed' when referring to him. Nowadays, this could be translated along the lines of 'Wiseman the Stupid Man', which is not exactly a flattering description for a head of state.

In spite of the overall failures of his reign, *Encyclopaedia Britannica* reveals that 'evidence from his charters and coinage suggest that Ethelred's government was more effective than was once believed.'

King Cnut tried to hold back the tide to prove he was all-powerful

IN the world of economics, eleventh-century King Cnut is regularly held up as a ridiculous figure who tried foolishly to stave off the inevitable. Historian and biographer M. J. Trow confirms in *Cnut* that 'the "Canute Syndrome" of self-delusion is regularly applied to politicians and economists.' Yet, in *Great Tales from History*, Robert Lacey suggests that 'history's mistake has been the belief that Cnut really did think he could stop the waves – according to Henry [of Huntingdon], the King thought quite the opposite.'

In his early twelfth-century work *Historia Anglorum*, chronicler Henry of Huntingdon describes the act as one of King Cnut's 'fine and magnificent deeds,' adding that 'before him, there had never been in England a king of such great authority.' He explains that when Cnut was 'at the height of his ascendancy, he ordered his chair to be placed on the sea-shore as the tide was coming in.' Huntingdon gives no indication where this piece of theatre took place, but *Breaking Butterflies* mentions 'a strong tradition in Sussex [that] favours the then important port of Bosham, much patronized by royalty and a popular point of embarkation.'

Huntingdon then describes Cnut announcing to the rising tide 'You are subject to me, as the land on which I am sitting is mine, and no one has resisted my overlordship with impunity. I command you, therefore, not to rise onto my land, nor to presume to wet the clothing or limbs of your master.' However, 'the sea came out as usual, and disrespectfully drenched the King's feet and shins.' Huntingdon explains that the King then cried out so that all his sycophantic courtiers could hear: 'Let all the world know that the power of kings is empty and worthless, and there is no king worthy of the name save Him by whose will heaven, earth and sea obey eternal laws.' The upshot of this demonstration of piety was that King Cnut 'never wore the golden crown on his neck [head], but placed it on the image of a crucified Lord, in eternal praise of God the

great king'. Cnut proved to his courtiers that he was powerless compared with God.

Just twenty years later, Anglo-Norman chronicler Geoffrey Gaimar's retelling in his mid-twelfth-century work *L'Estoire des Engles* locates the event on the River Thames and gives it a totally different slant. The King, finding 'he was disobeyed, and his command despised' stood where 'the tide was flowing near the church which is called Westminster'. Cnut held up his sceptre and said to the tide, 'Return back; flee from me, lest I strike thee,' but the King still got drenched. Gaimar records that he was 'duly humbled' and promised to make a pilgrimage to Rome.

In *The History of England* (Volume I), eighteenth-century historian David Hume redresses the balance yet again by following Huntingdon's interpretation, stating that Cnut answered his 'flatterers' by 'ordering his chair to be set on the sea-shore, while the tide was rising'. When he got soaked he remarked to them humbly that 'every creature in the universe was feeble and impotent' when compared with 'one Being alone', that of God.

During his reign, Cnut was generally well regarded. Jim Bradbury claims in *Medieval Warfare* that the tide story 'was later distorted to make Cnut appear arrogant'. Trow agrees, adding that the term 'Canute Syndrome' is applied 'in the modern world in a way completely opposed to the intentions of Henry of Huntingdon' whose description of the great King Cnut's 'piety and humility' has vanished. He is portrayed as a 'stupid and arrogant megalomaniac who believed that he had greater powers than God'. Perhaps wise King Cnut would have smiled philosophically at Gaimar's scandalous revision of his pious piece of theatre . . . or perhaps not.

Chapter 3

QUESTIONABLE QUEENS

Queen Elizabeth I had wooden teeth

THE sixteenth-century Virgin Queen was known for having a sweet tooth. Consequently, she finished up with practically no teeth at all. In *Elizabeth I*, Alison Plowden quotes contemporary German lawyer Paul Hentzner blaming the English predisposition to bad teeth on 'their inordinate fondness for sweetmeats'. Nor did it help that Elizabethan dental care was practically nonexistent. Elizabeth Jenkins explains in *Elizabeth the Great* that 'teeth were cleaned by rubbing them with a cloth inside and out,' and she records that 'the Queen's New Year gifts included holland tooth-cloths, edged with black and silver.'

The rot set in, so to speak, in Elizabeth I's middle years when her looks, though regal, were spoilt by decaying teeth. In his 1597 *Journal,* French ambassador André Hurault de Maisse describes Queen Elizabeth's teeth in 1596 as 'very yellow and unequal, compared with what people say they were formerly, and on the left side less than the right. Many of them are missing.' A consequence of her poor state of teeth, according to Maisse, was that 'one cannot understand her easily when she speaks quickly.'

A problematic lisp was not the worst of it. She also suffered from crippling bouts of toothache. In Elizabethan times, it appears that worms were considered not only the cause but also the cure for toothache. *Elizabeth's London* by Liza Picard quotes Thomas Hill's 1568 work *The Profitable Art of Gardening,* in which he suggests that powder of burnt rosemary wood was just the job to 'make the teeth white and flee [drive out] the worms in them'. She also refers to John Hollybush's unique recommendations in his 1561 *A Most Excellent and Perfect Homish Apothecary,* that toothache should be treated with 'grey worms . . . pierced together with a bodkin [needle]'.

One episode of toothache pained Queen Elizabeth for two months. Historian and biographer John Strype records in his 1701 work *Life and Acts of John Aylmer* that it 'forced her to pass whole nights without taking any rest'. The Queen would not agree to extraction since she was 'afraid of the acute pain that accompanied it', and was persuaded only after Bishop Aylmer nobly volunteered to have one of his own teeth extracted, so that she could see 'the pain was not so much, and not at all to be dreaded'.

By the time the Queen had reached her sixties, Plowden

quotes Hentzner describing what teeth she had left as 'black'. In *The Excruciating History of Dentistry,* James Wynbrandt quotes a witness in 1602, when the Queen was nearly seventy and at the end of her reign, commenting that she was 'still . . . frolicy and merry, only her teeth showeth some decay'. From eyewitness testimony, it seems clear that Elizabeth was clearly stuck with her own visibly rotting teeth, and she certainly hadn't requested the fashioning of a right royal pair of wooden teeth.

False teeth weren't invented until the eighteenth century and, until the advent of denture fixative, individual false teeth were purely for appearance and would have had to have been removed for eating. In the sixteenth century, rolled-up wads of cloth were generally employed to disguise the gaps. Wynbrandt's witness reveals that 'when she cometh in public [Elizabeth] putteth many fine cloths into her mouth to bear out her cheeks'. Plugs of rolled cloth used to fill toothless gaps could have resembled plugs of wood and so given rise to the myth.

Regular trips to the dentist don't seem such a bad option now when one considers the alternative.

Queen Boadicea rode a scythed chariot

THE first-century warrior queen, commonly known as Boadicea, was leader of the Iceni, an ancient British tribe from the area now known as East Anglia. She made war on her Roman oppressors after they appropriated her tribe's estates, flogged her and raped her two daughters.

Firstly, a word about her name. In *The Warrior Queens,* Antonia Fraser explains that first-century Roman historian

Tacitus gives the only contemporary rendering of the Queen's name as 'Boudicca'. However, she suggests that 'Tacitus . . . was in error' and that the correct spelling is 'Boudica'. Interestingly, Fraser points out the existence of an Old Welsh word *bouda* meaning victory, which suggests a strong link between 'Queen Boudica' and 'Queen Victoria'.

Thomas Thornycroft's striking bronze statue 'Boadicea and her Daughters', erected in 1902 on the embankment at Westminster, London shows the Queen, spear in hand, careering towards the foe. (Neither daughter appears to have redressed post-rape, but this doesn't seem to be affecting their focus.) Eminent archaeologist Graham Webster points out in *Boudica* that the chariot featured in the sculpture 'has a heavy metal body with solid wheels, unlikely to move far in muddy ground, even drawn by . . . large splendid and spirited horses'. He adds that 'the aspect which has seized popular fancy more than anything, is the pair of curved, vicious-looking knives fixed to the axles'. However, Fraser reveals that Boudica's chariot 'did not actually have knives (or scythes) affixed to its wheels', and goes on to assert that 'this is one of the very few statements which can be made with any certainty concerning her.' Webster agrees that this representation of Boudica's chariot is nothing more than 'a remarkable piece of romantic fiction'. While Miranda Green explains in *The Celtic World* that 'the presence of the scythes on the wheels do nothing to dispel the popular misconceptions surrounding the Celts; rather, they reinforce the legend from one generation to the next.' Webster suggests that 'this delightfully horrific detail will doubtless remain fixed in the public's mind as the image of the Britons and Boudica in particular.'

Thornycroft may have gained his inspiration from scythed chariots used in ancient Asia. In *Epitome of Military Science*, fourth-century writer Vegetius reveals that in the first century 'scythed chariots were used in battle by King Antiochus [of Syria] and Mithridates [King of Pontius].' Vegetius also confides that 'although at first they caused much alarm, they soon became a laughing stock' since 'when they came to battle, the Romans suddenly threw caltrops [four-spiked weapons] over the whole field. The speeding chariots were destroyed as they encountered them.' The effect was probably similar to throwing a modern-day police 'stinger' in front of a villain's four-by-four.

Third-century Persians also employed scythed chariots against Alexander the Great, but to no better effect. Rather than having their legs hacked off, Waldemar Heckel explains in *The Wars of Alexander the Great* that Alexander's 'javelin-men simply parted ranks upon their approach and shot down their drivers or their teams'.

As to the question of what ancient British chariots really looked like, Webster reveals that Caesar was in the habit of amusing his troops with tales of the 'British chariot' in action, which gives us an idea of the real nature of the vehicle: 'By daily exercises and use . . . [the charioteers] become so proficient that they drive their horses down the steepest slopes under complete control.' These skilled charioteers were able to 'stop and turn quickly, run along the pole, stand on the yoke and quickly back to the chariot'. It appears that first-century British charioteers relied considerably more on agility rather than fancy armaments, which may have looked impressive, but turned out to be completely useless.

Queen Cleopatra was a great beauty

FIRST-CENTURY BCE Macedonian Queen of Egypt, Cleopatra is famed for bewitching both Julius Caesar and later his general, Mark Antony, whom she eventually married. Her image on coins shows her to have had a long nose and a jutting chin. This contradiction is often explained by the suggestion that ideals of beauty change. It is argued

that long noses and jutting chins may have been fashionable during Cleopatra's time and now they are not. Despite the fact that first-century CE Roman historian Plutarch never met Cleopatra, in *The Lives of Noble Grecians and Romans* he provides the only detailed physical description we have of her. A careful reading of his description gives us the real answer: he suggests that her 'actual beauty . . . was not in itself so remarkable that none could be compared with her'. And nor was it, he claims, the kind where 'no one could see her without being struck by it'.

Cleopatra's beauty was – inconceivable to many modern-day minds – intellectual. Plutarch points out that it was not her features but her 'adroitness and subtlety in speech' that made the impact. He adds that Cleopatra met Antony 'when women's beauty is most splendid, and their intellects are in full maturity', and by this remark he appears to be saying that a woman's beauty improves with the development of her mind. Plutarch reveals that 'the contact of her presence, if you lived with her, was irresistible; the attraction of her person, joining with the charm of her conversation, and the character that attended all she said or did, was something bewitching . . . It was a pleasure merely to hear the sound of her voice, with which, like an instrument of many strings, she could pass from one language to another.' High praise indeed.

On the other hand, not everyone was quite so taken by her. In *The History of the Life of Marcus Tullius Cicero* by Conyers Middleton, Cicero (who lived opposite her) is quoted as saying that Cleopatra might have sent him over some quite acceptable books 'of a literary nature', but that did *not* excuse her swanning about in the gardens treating him with 'insolence'. Cicero declares that he could never think of it 'without indignation' and decided to 'have nothing therefore to do' with Antony and Cleopatra, since they clearly took him to have 'no feeling at all'.

Cicero seems to have had the last laugh, however, as the most recently discovered coin to depict Cleopatra has prompted some to claim that she resembled less a great beauty and looked more like the late, great . . . Les Dawson.

Queen Anne Boleyn had six fingers (and three breasts)

IN the sixteenth century, extra nipples, breasts or fingers marked the bearer out as a witch. Henry VIII would have been among the first to acknowledge that installing a witch-queen on the throne of England would have brought bad luck in the extreme, yet Henry and Anne Boleyn were married in 1533.

In *The Rise and Fall of Anne Boleyn*, Retha M. Warnicke states that any such assertions 'are absolutely false'. She explains that the instigator of the rumour was sixteenth-century Catholic activist Nicholas Sander, who claimed in his 1585 work *The Origin and Progress of the English Schism* that Anne had 'on her right hand, six fingers'. He also throws in 'a large wen [growth] under her chin', and claims that 'therefore to hide its ugliness, she wore a high dress covering her throat.' Sander also asserted that Anne's mother had been Henry VII's mistress, and that Henry had married his own daughter. His wealth of knowledge seems strange bearing in mind that when Anne was executed (in 1536), he would only have been six years old. Warnicke reveals that historians who were Sander's contemporaries, such as Edward Herbert and Gilbert Burnet (the Bishop of Salisbury), disputed Sander's accusations publicly.

In *The Life and Death of Anne Boleyn* by Eric Ives, we discover that at Anne's coronation in 1533, one hostile observer reported that 'she wore a violet velvet mantle with a high ruff to conceal a swelling in the neck, possibly a goitre.' Ives suggests that this was most likely 'wilful misinterpretation'.

If Anne had any physical anomalies, they amounted to no more than a minor malformation of her little fingertip and a mole or two. Biographer George Wyatt in his late-sixteenth-century work *Some Particulars of the Life of Queen Anne Boleigne* claims that 'there was found, indeed, upon the side of her nail, upon one of her fingers, some little show of a nail.' He adds that it was 'so small, by the report of those that have seen her, as the work master seemed to leave it an occasion of greater grace to her hand' and was 'usually by her hidden'. As to the moles, Wyatt suggests that 'likewise there were said to be upon some parts of her body, certain small moles incident to the clearest complexions'.

Regarding the charge of having three breasts, Ives states that contemporary Venetian diplomat Francesco Sanuto notes that Anne had 'a bosom not much raised'. Sanuto, when assiduously assessing Anne's anatomy, would surely have mentioned an extra breast. Shortly before their marriage Henry wrote to Anne, 'wishing myself (especially of an evening) in my sweetheart's arms, those pretty duckies I trust shortly to kiss . . .' Surely *he* would have noticed if there had been three such duckies?

It would appear that a small mole on Anne's neck or chest, according to some commentators, transformed first into a large wen, then a goitre and then magically (and thanks to Monsieur Percy's *Dictionaire des Science Medical*), into a third breast. A good trick if you can do it.

Queen Victoria's first name was Victoria

THE great Queen's first name occurs so frequently in history that we take its familiarity for granted. However, it was very nearly a different story and all due to the whims and fancies of a capricious uncle, the Prince Regent. *A*

Dictionary of First Names confirms that the first name of Queen Victoria was 'Alexandrina'.

In her biographical work *Victoria, R.I.,* Elizabeth Longford reveals that the royal baby, fifth in line to the throne, was to be christened 'Georgiana Charlotte Augusta Alexandrina Victoria'. Longford derived the account of the christening from a letter written by the child's mother, Victoria, Duchess of Kent.

Prince George, the Prince Regent, was the child's first godfather and Alexander I, Tsar of Russia, was her second (represented at the ceremony by the Duke of York). However, the first godfather hated the second, and the evening before the christening, the Prince Regent advised the parents in a curt telegram that 'the name Georgiana would not be used' as 'He did not chuse [sic] to place His name before the Emperor of Russia's.' He added that 'He could not allow it to follow.' As for the other names, he would speak to the child's parents about the matter.

On the day of the ceremony in 1819, Longford reveals that 'the Archbishop of Canterbury, baby in arms, stood waiting for the Prince Regent to pronounce the first name.' Nothing happened. Eventually, the Prince Regent gruffly proposed 'Alexandrina'. The Duke of Kent then prompted the Prince Regent for a second name, and Charlotte was suggested. As John Van der Kiste explains in *Childhood at Court 1819 to 1914*, Charlotte was the name of the Prince Regent's 'only child . . . [who] had died prematurely'. Van der Kiste surmises that since the Duke of Kent's child appeared strong and healthy, this may have been a source 'of bitterness and resentment on the part of the Prince Regent'. Thus, Charlotte was out of the question.

The Duke prompted the King to offer the name Augusta, but this was rejected, according to Longford, since it carried a 'suggestion of grandeur'. Eventually, the Prince Regent thundered 'Let her be called after her mother.' Van der Kiste adds that, annoyingly, he added the proviso that the name Victoria could not 'proceed to that of the Emperor'. And this is how the pride and joy of the Duke and Duchess of Kent became stuck with the only remaining option, that of Alexandrina Victoria. Van der Kiste adds that by this time, the child's mother 'was sobbing'.

Longford confirms that for the first nine years of her life, the princess was called 'by the foreign diminutive "Drina"'.

By the time she was eleven, her parents again attempted to alter her name to Charlotte or possibly Elizabeth since 'the two foreign names She bears are not suited to our national feeling.' However, the name Alexandrina gained a degree of acceptance since, as the *Concise Dictionary of World Place-Names* reveals, a lake in South Australia was named Alexandrina after the young princess.

Victoria herself had her own thoughts on the matter. Biographer Christopher Hibbert claims in *Queen Victoria* that although Victoria had been officially proclaimed 'our only lawful and rightful liege Lady Alexandrina Victoria', she 'never considered the possibility of being known as Queen Alexandrina'. Indeed Hibbert describes her omitting that name 'from all the documents which she was required to sign'. In *The Age of Reform 1815–70*, E. Llewellyn Woodward confirms that although documents prepared for publication describe her as 'Alexandrina Victoria', at her first Privy Council the Queen 'signed the register as "Victoria"'.

Even at Queen Victoria's coronation, the controversy surrounding her name continued. Longford confides that, at this time, 'Lord Melbourne was to tell Queen Victoria . . . that she had been called after the Tsar expressly to annoy the Prince Regent, who "HATED him; God damn him!"' And so the Alexandrinian era became the Victorian era.

Chapter 4

FALLACIOUS FOLK HEROES

Robin Hood lived in Sherwood Forest

A variety of candidates have been suggested as the original Robin Hood, but no particular historical figure has been positively identified as the good-hearted outlaw. In the *Oxford Dictionary of National Biography*, J. C. Holt reveals that a mid-thirteenth-century entry on the 'king's remembrancer's memoranda roll' of 1261 in Berkshire, pardons the Prior of Sandleford for 'seizing without warrant the chattels of William Robehod, fugitive'. While in *Imagining Robin Hood*, A. J. Pollard concludes that Robin Hood is 'essentially a fictional creation'.

The first surviving literary mention of Robin Hood is in the fourteenth century, when a character in William Langland's religious poem *Piers Plowman* claims 'I kan [know] rymes of Robyn Hood.' Holt maintains that the character of Maid Marian was introduced in the sixteenth century as 'a literary and dramatic figment'. Friar Tuck, however, was a real-life fifteenth-century Sussex parson named Robert Stafford. According to Holt, the reprobate parson headed a band that 'committed murders and robberies'.

The Robin Hood legend is invariably linked with Sherwood Forest in Nottinghamshire. Andrew Wyntoun's 1420 work *Orygynale Chronicle* states that 'Litil Iohun and Robert Hude' were 'Waythmen' [forest outlaws] who were 'commendit [commended] gud' in 'Ingilwode and Bernnysdaile' where they 'oyssit [practiced] al this tyme thar trawale [labour]'. This early mention has the 'gud' outlaws operating in either Barnsdale, Yorkshire or possibly in the Forest of Barnsdale in Rutland.

The *Gest of Robyn Hode*, an epic ballad compiled around thirty years after Wyntoun's work in 1450, supports this point, as it features the line: 'My name is Robin Hood of Barnesdale.' The 'proud sherif of Notingham' is also mentioned in the tales and Robin, though based in 'Barnesdale', states 'to day wil I to Notyngham', though when he is away 'Me longeth sore to Bernysdale'. (Barnsdale is spelt in a variety of ways in the ballad.) Holt suggests that 'the main setting of the *Gest of Robyn Hode* is Wentbridge and Barnsdale (West Riding)' in Yorkshire.

Perhaps the main reason that Robin Hood is believed to have come from Nottingham, and lived in Sherwood Forest, is thanks to the nineteenth-century writer Sir Walter Scott, who never let the facts get in the way of a good yarn. In his famous 1819 novel *Ivanhoe*, Scott places Robin firmly in twelfth-century Nottinghamshire by having him announce to King Richard I: 'Call me no longer Locksley, my Liege . . . I am Robin Hood of Sherwood Forest.' And so he has been ever since.

Frontiersman Daniel Boone was a ferocious 'Indian fighter'

EARLY American frontiersman Daniel Boone may have blazed a trail through the Appalachian Mountains (a traditional hunting ground for Native American Indians) in 1775 and made it possible for settlers to colonize Kentucky, but he did not achieve this by gunning down natives. In his biographical work *Daniel Boone: The Life and Legend of an American Pioneer*, John Mack Faragher claims that Boone's descendants 'always disputed claims that Boone was a ferocious fighter who had killed a great number of Indians'. Indeed, in interviews collected in *My Father: Daniel Boone*, Nathan Boone states that his father 'was only positive of killing . . . one'.

On this particular occasion, Boone had found himself hemmed in against the river, close to a lone Native American Indian, who was fishing from a fallen tree. Boone recounts how the Indian then 'tumbled into the river'. The implication was that the frontiersman had shot and killed the man in order to avoid detection, but was 'reluctant to admit it outright'. The man's death then 'opened an escape route for Boone'. Faragher explains that 'he was one of the few Indians that Boone acknowledged killing during his long lifetime on the frontier.' Nathan Boone also adds that his father 'believed he had killed Indians on other occasions,' meaning that possibly his bullets may have caused fatalities he had not specifically intended.

The Boone legend began with John Filson's 1784 book *The Adventures of Colonel Daniel Boon* (misspelling the subject's surname), a work that was incorporated in *The Discovery, Settlement and Present State of Kentucke*. Filson explains that would-be Kentucky settlers grew 'exceedingly disheartened' on account of being 'plundered, dispersed, and killed by the Indians, except Colonel Boon, who continued [as] an inhabitant of the wilderness'.

If Daniel Boone wasn't guilty of mowing down copious numbers of natives, surely he butchered a few bears? Two famous inscriptions carved on trees are attributed to him. One in Washington County, Tennessee reads 'D. Boon Cilled A. Bar on Tree in the year 1760.' The other one, now in the Museum of Filson Historical Society in

Louisville, states 'D. Boon Kilt a Bar, 1803.' Clearly Boone's spelling abilities hadn't improved over the forty-odd year interval. However, one would imagine he'd recall how to spell his own name. It's true that some eighteenth-century folk spelt their names differently on different occasions, but Faragher reveals that Boone 'always spelled his name with the final e' and claims that the 'semiliterate "Boon" is a tip-off of bogus inscriptions'.

Boone's recollections were embroidered by Timothy Flint, who, in his 1833 *Biographical Memoir of Daniel Boone, The First Settler of Kentucky,* adds bear fighting to Boone's achievements. Flint tells how Boone, having missed his shot at a 'she bear', took out his knife. The bear 'reared itself erect to grasp him with its huge paws' then obligingly 'pressed upon the knife until the whole blade was buried in its body' and 'fell harmless to the ground'. What a man . . .

Neither did Boone wear a racoon-skin cap. In *Daniel Boone Homestead,* Sharon Hernes Silverman reveals that 'Boone himself considered that style of headwear uncivilized.' He did, however, always insist on wearing a beaver hat. The racoon-skin cap legend arose when an actor, hired to play Boone in a minstrel show called *The Hunters of Kentucky,* was unable to find a beaver hat and used a racoon-skin cap instead.

According to Faragher, when Boone was asked if he ever became lost, the dauntless pioneer of the Wild West replied, 'I can't say as ever I was lost, but I was bewildered once for three days.' He was also, it would appear, a modest hero. Faragher quotes Boone stating that 'many heroic actions and chivalrous adventures are related of me which exist only in the regions of fantasy. With me the world has taken great liberties, and yet I have been but a common man.'

William Tell shot an apple on top of his son's head

FOURTEENTH-CENTURY Swiss folk hero William Tell is famous for firing a bolt from his crossbow into an apple placed on top of his son's head. Visitors to Altdorf in Switzerland can admire an impressive statue of William and son, dating him to 1307. According to the legend, Austrian tyrant Hermann Gessler, who was keen to demonstrate his authority, erected a 'lofty pole' in Altdorf marketplace bearing his cap. Every villager was required to, as nineteenth-century German dramatist Friedrich von Schiller puts it, 'do it reverence with bended knee'. William Tell refused and as punishment was ordered to 'take thy bow . . . [and] shoot an apple from the stripling's [his son's] head!' Tell accomplished the feat, but rather rashly confessed that 'if that my hand had struck my darling child, this

second arrow [bolt] I had aimed at you, and, be assured, I should not then have miss'd.' A chase ensued and Tell killed the wicked Gessler with a bolt from his trusty crossbow.

Happily, though, no Swiss infant was actually subjugated to this scary feat, since *Encyclopaedia Britannica* informs us that 'there is no evidence . . . for the existence of Tell.'

In Jonathan Steinberg's *Why Switzerland?* we learn that 'the first full account of the story appeared in *White Book of Sarnen*,' which dates from 1474. *Merriam-Webster's Encyclopedia of Literature* suggests that the classic form of the legend appears in Gilg Tschudi's eighteenth-century *Chronicon Helveticum.* In an 1804 copy of Schiller's play *William Tell*, the preface explains that the tale was based on a 'worldwide legend which became localized in Switzerland in the fifteenth century'. The story of the rebel Tell became 'incorporated into the history of the struggle of the Forest Cantons for deliverance from Austrian domination'. These events supposedly helped spur the people to rise up against Austrian rule.

The story became even more famous in 1829, when Italian composer Gioacchino Rossini based an opera on Schiller's tale. The complete work is rarely performed nowadays since it can run to six hours.

The legendary William Tell wasn't showing off his skill as a marksman, of course, as he had been *forced* to shoot the apple from his son's head and his fine marksmanship won the day. Unfortunately, the same cannot be said of US novelist William S. Burroughs who, in 1951, in a state of intoxication, accidentally shot and killed his second wife Joan with a loaded gun while staging a William Tell act using a drinking glass. This illustrates the point that it is *always* a mistake to place any sort of target on your head in the presence of a drunken novelist with a firearms fascination – a salutary lesson to us all.

Paul Revere rode to Concord crying 'The British are coming!'

AMERICAN folk hero Paul Revere's famous ride occurred at the outset of the American Revolutionary War. In *The Road to Yorktown*, military historian John Selby explains that British general Thomas Gage received orders to 'deal with the rebellion'. On 18 April 1775, he issued secret instructions to 'seize and destroy . . . artillery [and] ammunition' at Concord while taking care not to 'plunder the inhabitants, or hurt private property'. However, that evening he was aghast to learn that the whole town was whispering of how the redcoats would 'miss their aim [goal]' – his American-born wife, it would appear, had shared the intelligence with the locals, revealing divided loyalties. This put Gage in an awkward position, but he decided to continue with the expedition even though he knew the munitions would be gone – perhaps hoping to make a show of capturing some artillery. In *A Few Bloody Noses*, Robert Harvey describes this as 'a disastrous miscalculation'.

Paul Revere is often portrayed as selflessly galloping through the countryside warning of the imminent arrival of the redcoats, but he was simply doing his job. In a 1798 letter to Jeremy Belknap, Revere explains, 'I was imployed by the Select men of the Town of Boston . . . to Carry their dispatches to New York and Philadelphia for Calling a Congress.' Fellow dissidents John Hancock and Samuel

Adams were thought (mistakenly) to be the objects of the military expedition. Revere was sent along with dispatch rider William Dawes to Lexington, rather than Concord, to warn the pair of their imagined imminent arrest.

Nearly a hundred years later, in 1863, Henry Wadsworth Longfellow immortalized this ride in a ballad entitled *Paul Revere's Ride*, which begins 'Listen, my children, and you shall hear / Of the midnight ride of Paul Revere.' This is where fact and fiction blur. Longfellow claims that Revere waited for lantern signals 'One if by land, and two if by sea / And I on the opposite shore will be / Ready to ride and spread the alarm / Through every Middlesex village and farm.' But the *Concise Oxford Companion to American Literature* reveals that 'Revere never waited for signals from lanterns.' Revere, in his letter, explains that the signals were *from* him not *to* him. He would 'shew . . . Lanthorns in the North Church Steeple . . . as a Signal; for we were aprehensive it would be dificult to Cross the Charles River, or git over Boston neck'. As George F. Scheer and Hugh F. Rankin explain in *Rebels and Redcoats,* Revere 'would endeavour to reach Charlestown with details, but if he should fail, the lanterns would tell the colonel what warning he must send into the countryside'.

On his ride Revere tells how, in Medford, he 'awaked the Captain of the Minute men . . . and . . . alarmed almost every House, till I got to Lexington' where he 'alarmed Mr Adams and Col. Hancock'. Revere was reprimanded by the guard for being too noisy. In *Paul Revere's Ride,* David Hackett Fischer records that Revere replied, 'Noise! . . . You'll have noise enough before long! The Regulars are coming out!' This appears to be the origin of the much-

quoted phrase 'The British are coming.' Fischer points out that 'express riders that night would speak of Regulars, Redcoats, the King's men, and even the "Ministerial Troops" if they had been to college.' However, he adds that 'no messenger is known on good authority to have cried, "The British are coming"' for the simple reason that 'in 1775, the people of Massachusetts still thought that they were British.' Fischer describes colonial Jason Russell, who, when asked why he was preparing to defend his house from attack, stated that 'an Englishman's home is his castle.'

In Lexington, Revere, Dawes (who turned up belatedly), Adams and Hancock realized that the British military expedition was too large for the arrest of just two dissidents. (*Encyclopaedia Britannica* confirms that 'the troops made no effort to find them.') So they correctly surmised that the soldiers were heading for the munitions in Concord. Revere, Dawes and Dr Samuel Prescott rode towards Concord 'to secure the Stores, &c. there ... I likewise mentioned, that we had better allarm all the Inhabitents till we got to Concord'.

In Longfellow's ballad, Revere reaches his goal: 'It was two by the village clock / When he came to the bridge in Concord town.' In reality, Revere and Dawes were inter-cepted by British troops and never did reach Concord. An entry in *The Oxford Companion to United States History* explains that 'Revere was detained for several hours.' Both Dawes and Revere lost their horses: Revere's was taken by a 'Sargent of Grenadiers' who considered it an improvement upon his own. Both men returned to Lexington on foot. Revere records that Prescott 'jumped his Horse over a low Stone wall'. It was Prescott who 'got to Concord'. (*Listen, my children, for what I've got / Is the more accurate tale of Sam Prescott ...*)

It is generally claimed that Revere's hasty gallop bought the Lexington colonials precious time to prepare for the arrival of the redcoats. However, Robert Harvey states that Revere warned the revolutionists 'prematurely'. They turned out soon after Revere's arrival, but as Selby explains, the British soldiers were still some hours away so the men were dismissed 'with instructions to assemble again later directly they heard the beat of the drum'.

At dawn, Gage's redcoats finally arrived at Lexington. In James Kendall Hosmer's 1886 biography *Samuel Adams the Man of the Town-Meeting*, he describes Adams 'flying with Hancock across the fields from Lexington to Woburn' to the safety of a friend's house exclaiming 'What a glorious morning is this!'

Back at Lexington, glory was in rather sort supply. Both sides were on strict instructions not to fire first. *The Great American History Fact-Finder* reveals that 'no one knows who fired the first shot.' Harvey describes it as 'one of those terrible accidents that happen when jittery troops come within range of each other.' Both sides suffered casualties, and the colonials, outnumbered, retreated. The redcoats continued unhindered onto the bloody Battle of Concord.

Chapter 5

SPURIOUS STATESMEN

Abraham Lincoln wrote the Gettysburg Address on the back of an envelope

FOUR months after the Battle of Gettysburg, fought in July 1863 during the American Civil War, a funeral service was held for the lost soldiers. Massachusetts orator Edward Everett was asked to deliver the oration. The US President Abraham Lincoln was invited at the last moment. To everyone's surprise, the President agreed to attend and even offered to say a few words. *The Oxford Companion to*

United States History dispels as 'a myth' the claim that Lincoln scribbled down his speech on the back of an envelope on his way to the service, suggesting that the idea derives from 'contrasting Lincoln's short (three-minute) speech with Everett's laboured two-hour performance'.

In *Gettysburg Battlefield*, David J. Eicher agrees that the speech was 'not penned on an envelope en route'. Indeed, Eicher reveals that 'five . . . copies in Lincoln's hand' exist and none of them are written on the back of an envelope. He explains that Lincoln 'wrote the draft of his speech in Washington'.

It is also sometimes suggested that Lincoln's speech was only hailed as a success in hindsight. Norman Hapgood's *Abraham Lincoln* reveals Lincoln's disappointment with the lack of fervour in the applause at the end. It seems that he commented to a companion 'It is a flat failure. The people are disappointed.' Yet, the *Companion to United States History* reports that Lincoln's speech was 'interrupted by applause five times'.

Samuel Flagg Bemis's *The American Secretaries of State and their Diplomacy* reveals that Everett himself wrote to Lincoln afterwards, stating 'I wish that I could flatter myself that I had come as near to the central idea of the occasion in two hours as you did in two minutes.' In *The Life and Letters of John Hay*, Lincoln's personal secretary William Roscoe Thayer records Hay stating that 'the President, in a fine, free way, with more grace than is his wont, said his half dozen words of consecration, and the music wailed and we went home through crowded and cheering streets.' The audience, having just sat through Everett's two-hour offering (unremembered now, as Hapgood points out), possibly couldn't quite believe that Lincoln's was over in just three minutes. In other words, the audience wasn't sure whether to make their final applause because they didn't know if he had finished.

Brevity clearly served Lincoln well in this situation, but not to the extent that he could have drafted his speech on the back of an envelope.

Benito Mussolini made the trains run on time

AFTER the First World War, the ailing Italian railway system received new investment. The claim was, according to biographer Denis Mack Smith in *Mussolini*, that during the 1920s 'Italian trains were the envy of all Europe' as 'Mussolini did his best to make the train service into a symbol of fascist efficiency.' The alleged improvement was noticed by the Infanta Eulalia of Spain who, in her 1925 book *Courts and Countries after the War*, suggests that 'the first benefit of Benito Mussolini's direction in Italy begins to be felt when one crosses

the Italian Frontier and hears "*Il treno arriva all'orario.*" ["The train is arriving on time."]' Indeed, *The Oxford Dictionary of Modern Quotations* describes Mussolini famously instructing a stationmaster 'We must leave exactly on time . . . From now on everything must function to perfection.'

However, as is common with many politicians, the execution of high ideals often results in a triumph of appearance over achievement. According to Peter Neville in *Mussolini*, 'the groundwork on the railways had in fact been carried out before 1922,' the year that Mussolini came to power. Even with the supposed improvements, Mack Smith reveals that 'some travellers reported that the celebrated trains running invariably on time were, to some extent at least, a convenient myth'. In *The Golden Age Is In Us*, Alexander Cockburn quotes US investigative journalist George Seldes in 1936, reporting that 'while the big express trains were mostly on schedule (though other travellers disputed even this) the local trains had huge delays.'

Cockburn suggests that 'millions of commuters round the world laud Il Duce's memory' simply because 'Mussolini's PR men fanned the legend'. Mack Smith agrees that Mussolini's 'propaganda was very successful', while Neville gives railway efficiency improvement as one example of Mussolini's 'spectacular over-hyped success'. What is more, Cockburn claims that 'Mussolini also took care to ban all reporting of railway accidents and delays.' When it came to improving the railways, it would appear that the only thing Mussolini really succeded in doing was hoodwinking the Spanish Infanta.

Winston Churchill was born in a ladies' lavatory

THE parents of British Prime Minister Winston Churchill – American socialite Jennie Jerome and Lord Randolph Churchill – had a whirlwind romance. In *Churchill: A Biography,* Roy Jenkins explains that the couple 'first met at a Cowes regatta shipboard party on 12 August 1873 and became engaged to be married three days later'. They were married at the British Embassy in Paris on 15 April the following year. Seven and a half months later, on 30 November 1874, baby Winston was born. Not surprisingly, his date of birth has given rise to speculation that he was conceived *before* the wedding, although it is of course possible that he was born six weeks' premature.

In *The Titled Americans,* Elisabeth Kehoe quotes a letter from Lord Randolph Churchill to his mother-in-law, Clara (said to be of Iroquois descent, according to the *Oxford Dictionary of National Biography*), noting that Jennie had 'no chloroform' and stating the hope that the 'baby things' would come 'with all speed' since they were having to borrow them from 'the Woodstock Solicitor's wife'. The sense of mild panic in the letter suggests that Winston's birth had come as a surprise even to his mother.

It is sometimes said that there are two conflicting accounts of Churchill's birth, but they are simply two halves of the same account differently related. All biographers agree that Churchill was born at Blenheim Palace, Oxfordshire, the ancestral family home of Lord Randolph's family. (The couple were staying there while their London flat was being finished ready for the birth.) The question is: which room?

The most popular version of events relates that Jennie, while attending a ball, delivered prematurely in the ladies' loo. (Jennie would no doubt have welcomed such a speedy delivery: she was, in fact, in labour for around twenty-four gruelling hours.)

The second account is based on Lord Randolph's letter to his mother-in-law, which states, as Jenkins relates, that Jennie 'had a fall on Tuesday walking with the shooters, and a rather imprudent and rough drive in a pony carriage brought on the pains on Saturday night. We tried to stop them, but it was no use.' Jenkins goes on to add that 'neither the London obstetrician nor his Oxford auxiliary could arrive in time, although it was over twenty-four hours to the birth from the onset of labour pains.' He added that 'the baby was born very early on the Monday morning with the assistance only of the Woodstock country doctor.' There is no mention here of a hasty delivery in any sort of lavatory.

In *The Last Lion*, William Manchester ties the two accounts together by explaining that on the Saturday night after the fall on the Tuesday, as mentioned by Lord Churchill, Jennie insisted on attending the 'annual St Andrew's ball [which] was held in the Palace'. (Possibly, Lord Randolph diplomatically substituted the 'imprudent carriage ride' for the 'imprudent party-going' in the letter to his mother-in-law.) Manchester explains that Jennie was 'on the floor, pirouetting, when the pains started'. He claims that she headed for her bedroom but 'fainted and was carried into a little room just off Blenheim Great Hall'. In *A History of the County of Oxford* (Volume 12) the 'little room' is describes as the Dean Jones room, which was a 'little apartment' west of the Great Hall and was acting, for the evening, as 'the ladies' cloakroom' to house the 'velvet capes and feather boas' of the female guests. The term cloakroom – originally a room for housing outer garments – is nowadays often used as a euphemism for the room containing the WC. So, we can see how the little apartment transmuted into the ladies' cloakroom and then the ladies' loo.

In truth, Sir Winston Churchill was born early one Monday morning in a well-appointed, self-contained apartment in Blenheim Palace with the local doctor in attendance. Churchill, when quizzed about the circumstances of his arrival, would famously comment 'Although present on that occasion, I have no clear recollection of the events leading up to it.'

Nelson had a death wish at the Battle of Trafalgar

IT has been said that British naval commander Viscount Horatio Nelson made up his mind to die abroad his ship, the *Victory,* in 1805 during the Battle of Trafalgar against the French. This was apparently evident because, on the morning of the engagement, Nelson appeared in a frock coat with 'aim here' stars sewn onto the left breast. Apparently, the ship's surgeon Dr William Beatty, who was about to remonstrate with him on this matter, was ordered by Nelson, along with all officers not stationed on deck, to return to his quarters. Nelson is then said to have paraded about the deck positively inviting a sniper's bullet.

In *The Dispatches and Letters of Vice Admiral Lord Viscount Nelson,* flag captain Thomas Masterman Hardy states that Nelson 'dressed himself in the same Coat which

he had commonly worn since he left Portsmouth; it was a plain blue Coat, on which the Star of the Bath was embroidered, as was then customary.' In the same volume, Beatty reports that Lord Nelson was 'dressed as usual in his Admiral's frock coat, bearing on the left breast four stars of different orders, which he always wore with his common apparel.' Presumably, since Nelson *was* shot by a French sniper in precisely the manner related by the tale, it is tempting to imagine that Nelson intended this all along.

A. M. Rodger's entry in the *Oxford Dictionary of National Biography* reveals that 'there is no evidence that he deliberately sought or recklessly courted death.' In *Horatio Nelson*, Tom Pocock adds that there is no doubt that he looked forward to his return, having written to daughter Horatia two days earlier: 'I shall be sure of your prayers for my safety . . . and speedy return to dear Merton.'

Pocock solves the puzzle by explaining that the 'aim here' stars were 'inconspicuous cloth replicas of his decorations'. At that time, it was usual for knights to wear their insignias at all times. The four embroidered stars were a time-saving measure: rather than fixing medals to the coat, the coat was permanently embroidered with the stars, which represented the decorations. In fact, in *Dispatches and Letters*, Hardy rather than Beatty is quoted as pointing out that the decorations might mark Nelson out as a target.

Nelson, in his no-nonsense manner, replied that he was aware that the decorations 'might be seen, but it was now too late to be shifting a coat'. If Nelson had been more concerned with his outfit than with the French onslaught, the battle might have had a very different outcome:

– 'Lord Nelson, the French are upon us!'
– 'Give me five more minutes, Hardy. I might go with the full dress frock coat after all.'

Napoleon Bonaparte was short in stature

MUCH is made of the late-eighteenth-century French Emperor Napoleon's supposed short stature. Biographies often describe him standing at just 5 foot 2 inches. In his 1910 work *Memoirs of Napoleon Bonaparte*, French biographer Claude François Méneval states that 'Napoleon was of mediocre stature (about 5 foot 2 inches), and well built.'

In *No Ordinary General* by Desmond Gregory, British contemporary Sir Henry Bunbury describes Napoleon in later life as '5 foot 6 inches high'. English observer Joseph Farington in *The Farington Diary 1923–8* wrote in 1802 that Napoleon's 'person is below middle size. I do not think him more than 5 foot 6 inches', while a colleague of his considered Napoleon to be 5 foot 7 inches high. In Jean Duhamel's *The Fifty Days: Napoleon in England,* the author claims that Napoleon was 'about 5 foot 6 inches, and . . . stockily built'.

Why the discrepancy in the French and English heights? The clue lies in the footnote in a book compiled by his private secretary, Louis Antoine Fauvelet de Bourrienne, which details a 1784 school report concerning fifteen-year-old Napoleon: 'to wit, M. de Buonaparte (Napoleon), born 15th of August, 1769: in height 4 feet, 10 inches, 10 lines.' It states that the cited measurement was in French feet, and at the beginning of the nineteenth century, French feet and inches were longer than English ones. Campbell Morfit's 1847 work *Chemistry Applied to the Manufacture of Soap and Candles*, cites a French foot as equivalent to 1.066 of an English foot, likewise inches. (Lines, subsections of an inch, were equal to 0.0888 of the English equivalent.) By this convention, Napoleon's height at fifteen was 5 foot 3 inches in English measurements, which is an inch taller than he was said, by some, to have stood as an adult.

After Napoleon's death in 1821, his height was officially recorded at 5 foot 2 inches in French feet, which makes Napoleon's adult height 5 foot 6 inches by English standards. The average male height in France at the time was 5 foot 5 inches (Englishmen were slightly taller), which therefore makes the French Emperor slightly above average. Napoleon wasn't a particularly tall man, but neither was he especially short. He was, as Méneval correctly states, 'of mediocre stature': unless the deceased Napoleon, having died under British rule, was measured with a British rule . . .

Chapter 6

FELONIOUS FEMALES

Lady Godiva rode naked through the streets of Coventry

ANGLO-SAXON Lady Godiva (or more accurately 'Godgifu') lived in eleventh-century Mercia (the Midlands) and was the wife of Leofric, Earl of Mercia. The Anglo-Saxon name *Godgifu* means 'God's gift'. She certainly lives up to her name in John Collier's late-nineteenth-century painting, which depicts her astride her horse with her fabled long hair failing to cover anything at all.

In *Breaking Butterflies*, Robert Gambles explains that 'most mediaeval chroniclers avidly noted down any "sensational" item of "news" that came their way.' Yet, as Daniel Donoghue notes in his informative work *Lady Godiva*, for more than a century after Godiva's death (in 1080), 'no written source makes even the faintest allusion to a legendary ride or to anything now commonly associated with it, such as nakedness, the horse, or taxation.' The *Penguin Biographical Dictionary of Women* claims that 'there is no factual basis for this ride and no contemporary evidence that she ever visited Coventry.'

In the eighth volume of *A History of the County of Warwick*, the legend is said to originate from thirteenth-century chronicler Roger of Wendover. In his prettily titled 1235 work *Flowers of History,* he records the goodly deeds of Leofric and his pious wife Godiva, and refers to Leofric's death and burial in 1057. But when the story of Godiva's horseback ride is disclosed, the demise of Leofric appears to be forgotten. According to Roger, 'the Countess Godiva' longed 'to free the town of Coventry from the oppression of a heavy toll', but the erstwhile goodly Leofric (who had died in the book's previous paragraph) was having none of it. Thus, Godiva 'with a woman's pertinacity, never ceased to exasperate her husband on that matter' until at last he challenged her to mount her horse 'and ride naked, before all the people, through the market . . . and on your return you shall have your request'. Leofric presumed that would be an end to the matter, but 'the Countess, beloved of God . . . let down her tresses, which covered the whole of her body like a veil, and then mounted her horse and attended by two knights, she rode through the market-place, without being seen, except her fair legs.' Good to his word, Leofric 'freed the town of Coventry and its inhabitants from the aforesaid service'. Gambles suggests that this tale may have been based on a lost chronicle written by Geoffrey, Prior of the monastery of Coventry between 1216 and 1235.

Fourteenth-century English chronicler and monk Ranulf Higden in his work *Polychronicon* explains that Leofric, at his wife's request, 'made his citee Coventre fre of all toll out take of hors [except for horses]'. And to go for the full house, Godiva 'rood naked, thro the middes of the cite in a

morowe, covered but with here awne here'. In *Grafton's Chronicles,* sixteenth-century chronicler Richard Grafton added that 'every person should [remain] shut in their houses.' *A History of the County of Warwick* notes that a seventeenth-century ballad says someone 'let down a window' whereupon Godiva's horse neighed. The tax exemption in this version was given for all *but* horses.

Gambles reveals that if the tax in question was King Harthacnut's 'heregeld', Leofric would not have had the authority to abolish it. If, on the other hand, it was a local tax, 'Coventry was Godiva's own estate' and because 'she alone . . . had the right to levy a tax on the town . . . she had no cause to plead with her husband as the chronicle describes.' *Encyclopaedia Britannica* goes further, stating that an enquiry showed at the time that 'no tolls were paid in Coventry except on horses.' Perhaps the whole tale came about in order to explain the unfathomable state of horse taxation in eleventh-century Coventry.

In later versions of the story, the legend of 'Peeping Tom' arose from claims that one of the townsfolk looked at Lady Godiva during her ride through Coventry, instead of averting his eyes, and as a punishment he was struck blind. When the Reverend Rowland Davies was recorded as visiting the city in 1690, he noted an 'image of an old man looking out of the window' at the end of Broadgate, which had been erected 'in memory of a fellow who peeped out there when the Queen rode naked through the town'.

In summary, *A History of the County of Warwick* suggests that 'the origin of the Godiva story and procession lies in pagan myth and ritual rather than in an act by the historic Countess Godiva.'

Mata Hari was an accomplished First World War spy

MATA HARI was executed by a French firing squad during the First World War on the charge of being a spy. However, the most infamous female spy of all time discovered no useful information and was probably no more than a high-class courtesan.

Dutch-born Margaretha Geertruida Zelle had an unsuccessful career as a teacher and a failed marriage to an army captain. In 1905, Margaretha took to exotic dancing in Paris under the stage name of Mata Hari, which is said to be a Malay expression for the sun, meaning 'eye of the dawn'. A tall, attractive woman, vaguely familiar with East Indian dancing and unconcerned about appearing virtually nude in public, she became an instant success.

When her dancing career began to wane, she fell back on selling sexual favours to European military officers and politicians, and during these liaisons was apparently asked a number of times to act as a spy. In *The Enemy Within,* Terry Crowdy reveals that 'despite her being under constant surveillance, the French could find no evidence against her.'

According to Morton S. Freeman in *A New Dictionary of Eponyms,* in 1917 'the prosecutor at her trial claimed that her spying had caused the deaths of at least 50,000 Frenchmen,' even though there was no corroborating proof to support the claim. Ultimately, despite having citizenship in a neutral country, she was found guilty of espionage and faced the death penalty.

Philip's World Encyclopedia agrees that 'although her conduct was suspicious, few people now believe she was the mysterious secret agent that the French authorities alleged.' Her MI5 file notes, released in 1999, state that there was no evidence that she passed on any information of military importance.

The Mammoth Book of War Correspondents records Paris staff correspondent Henry G. Wales describing how, at her execution, 'Mata Hari was not bound and she was not blindfolded. She stood gazing steadfastly at her executioners . . . their rifles were at their shoulders; each man gazed down his barrel at the breast of the women which was the target. She did not move a muscle.' The sound of the volley rang out. 'At the report Mata Hari fell.' It appears that she did not blow kisses to her executioners, as is sometimes claimed, but that she did die with admirable composure, which was surprising for someone who had been tried and condemned without any real evidence being produced to confirm her guilt.

Florence Nightingale nursed wounded soldiers in the Crimea

FLORENCE NIGHTINGALE first visited the battlefields of the Crimea in 1854, to try to set up field hospitals, and it was there that she became involved with the war effort. However, she did most of her hospital work in Scutari, close to Constantinople [Istanbul], about 200 miles from the battlefront. In the preface of her 1863 work *Notes on Hospitals*, she wrote that 'it may seem a strange principle to enunciate as the very first requirement in a Hospital that it should do the sick no harm,' but adopting this important point of view, she improved hospital hygiene and cut mortality rates from 42 per cent down to 2 per cent. Florence achieved this great feat through organization and administration: she did little actual nursing.

In 1845, the young, well-to-do Florence, wishing to nurse, requested to attend a local infirmary in Salisbury, but was prevented from doing so because her parents refused to give their permission. In an 1896 letter to Mrs Charles Roundell, Florence, recalling how she had searched for accredited nurse training, complained that 'there was none to be had in England.' In 1850, she attended the Institution of Protestant Deaconesses at Kaiserswerth in Germany for three months

where it is often claimed that she received a full training. However, Florence, in her letter, explains that she 'took all the training that was to be had', but complained that while the vegetable gardening was directed by a 'very capable sister . . . the nurse [nursing] was nil, [and] the hygiene horrible.'

Florence then visited Paris, but according to Lucille A. Joel in *Professional Nursing*, her efforts to 'study with the Sisters of Charity in Paris were frustrated, although she got permission to inspect the hospitals.' In 1853, Joel explains that Nightingale gained an unpaid post as 'Superintendent of a charity hospital (probably more of a nursing home) for ill governesses run by titled ladies.' *The Oxford Companion to British History* reveals that 'her real talents lay in administration, where she could manipulate and assert her will.' Thus, Florence set about 'making herself an expert on hospital administration'. At this point, Sidney Herbert, Secretary of War and an old friend, suggested she take nurses to the Crimea and employ her much-needed 'power of administration' to improve conditions there.

Florence's administration worked miracles in Scutari. In 1855, a *Times* correspondent reported that 'when all the medical officers have retired for the night and silence and darkness have settled down upon those miles of prostrate sick, she may be observed alone, with a little lamp in her hand, making her solitary rounds.' Poet Henry Longfellow further immortalized Florence in his 1857 work *Santa Filomena*: 'Lo! in that hour of misery / A lady with a lamp I see / Pass through the glimmering gloom, / And flit from room to room.' There is no mention in either description of nursing, but simply of inspection.

A far better example of a Crimean War nurse is Jamaican Mary Seacole. Mary sailed to England, as she explains in her autobiography *Wonderful Adventures of Mary Seacole in Many Lands,* 'to offer myself . . . as a recruit' for Florence Nightingale's nursing vanguard. Unfortunately, she did not gain an audience with Florence, and a recruiting nurse told her that her offer to help in the Crimea 'could not be entertained'. So she tried a different recruiting nurse, but 'read in her face . . . that, had there been a vacancy, I should not have been chosen to fill it.' Bemused by her apparent unsuitability, she wondered if 'these ladies shrink from accepting my aid because my blood flowed beneath a somewhat duskier skin than theirs?'

Undaunted, Mary financed her own passage to the Crimea and as *The Times* correspondent William Howard Russell explains in his 1856 work *The War*, five miles from the battle front, 'between the Col de Balaklava and Kadikoi, Mrs Seacole . . . has pitched her abode . . . and . . . doctors and cures all manner of men with extraordinary success.' Mary reveals that she was often 'under-fire'. In the same year, an Adjutant-General (as quoted in her autobiography) wrote a letter of recommendation, stating 'this excellent woman exerted herself in . . . attending the wounded men, even in positions of danger, and in assisting sick soldiers by all means in her power.'

Florence Nightingale was doubtless a fine hospital administrator, but it's Mary Seacole who comes closer to the image of the front-line, hands-on nurse we invariably, but rather mistakenly, associate with the name of Nightingale.

Grand Duchess Anastasia of Russia escaped the Bolshevik massacre

ANASTASIA was the youngest daughter of Tsar Nicholas II, the last Emperor of Russia. The Tsar and his family were executed in a cellar in Yekaterinburg where they had been imprisoned by Bolsheviks following the October Revolution in 1918.

Pavel Medvedev was a Bolshevik guard who was present during the event. His testimony, included in Marc Ferro's

Nicholas II, states that 'at midnight Commandant Yurovsky . . . woke up the Tsar's family . . . Yurovsky ordered me: "Go into the street, see if there is anybody there, and wait and check whether the shots are heard."' Medvedev explains that he 'went out into the yard . . . and before I got to the street I heard firing. I turned back immediately (only two or three minutes had elapsed) and . . . saw that all the members of the Tsar's family were lying on the floor with many wounds in their bodies.'

After the executions, numerous Anastasias came forward to lay claim to the Romanov fortune. The principal candidate was 'Anna Anderson', whose story was believed by many people. At about the same time that Anna Anderson materialized, a Polish factory worker by the name of Franziska Schanzkowska went missing, which led to suspicions that the two women were one and the same. Anna Anderson's court hearing began in 1938, lasted for over thirty years, and resulted in no conclusive findings. In 1970, courts in Germany rejected her claims once and for all.

Meanwhile, the tale of a surviving Anastasia prompted French dramatist Marcelle-Maurette to pen her 1954 play *Anastasia*. Two years later, the American film version starred Ingrid Bergman, who won an Academy Award for her poignant performance in the title role.

In 1984, the advent of DNA fingerprinting made it possible for Anna Anderson's claim to be genetically tested at last. Strangely, Anna refused to submit to any tests, died the same year and left instructions for her remains to be cremated. It seemed that the mystery would remain unsolved until it was discovered that before her death Anna had had an operation, and the hospital still had useable tissue samples. In the 1990s, DNA from the samples was compared with DNA taken from Prince Philip (a distant relative of the Tsar on his mother's side) and samples of the Romanov bones. DNA expert Dr Peter Gill concluded that Anna's sample 'did not match the DNA profile, which we would expect ... from the grand Duchess Anastasia'. What was more, the maternal grand-nephew of Franziska Schanzkowska provided a sample for DNA comparison with that of Anna Anderson, and Dr Gill pronounced 'a positive match'.

Most authorities agree that Anastasia died in the cellar with the rest of her family. Yet a few still hold to the belief that Anastasia survived the massacre, thus proving that the power of fable is great when it comes to the legacy of a murdered princess.

Mrs Beeton was an expert cook

IF you pictured the venerated Victorian cookbook writer as a plump housewife, jotting down her expertise at the end of a distinguished career, think again. Slender, newly married, twenty-year-old Isabella Beeton began compiling *Book of Household Management* in 1857 as a business and journalistic exercise. In *A Magazine of Her Own?*, Margaret Beetham explains that, in 1856, Isabella married *The Englishwoman's Domestic Magazine* publisher Sam Beeton, and it was this monthly journal that featured many of the recipes and articles which would later be incorporated into Isabella's book.

She states in the preface that the work, which was published in 1861, took 'four years' incessant labour'. On page iii of *Household Management*, Isabella opines that 'I must frankly own, that if I had known, beforehand, that this book would have cost me the labour which it has, I should never have been courageous enough to commence it.' This may have been because, as Lorna Sage reveals in *Women's Writing in English*, Isabella 'knew little about practical cooking and employed a cook'. Mrs Beeton makes no secret of her being 'indebted, in some measure, to many correspondents of the *Englishwoman's Domestic Magazine* who have obligingly placed at my disposal their formulae for many original preparations.' Indeed, rather than claiming authorship, the book is described on the frontispiece as

being merely 'edited by Mrs Isabella Beeton'. She also mentions her 'diligent study of the works of the best modern writers on cookery', though she falls short of naming them. Sage confirms that many of the recipes were 'culled from the better books such as Eliza Acton's'. Regardless of the sources used and Mrs Beeton's lack of practical expertise, 60,000 copies of her *Book of Household Management* were sold in the first year.

Among some of the tips she mentions in the book, Isabella warns against serving guinea pig since 'their flesh, although edible, is decidedly unfit for food' and she advises that they are 'as useless as they are harmless'. Isabella reveals that swan 'is now rarely seen upon the table' although she suspects they still serve it in Norwich. Although Lorna Sage notes that 'Isabella claimed to have tested all the recipes', on page vi there appears a list of errata including an amendment to the recipe for Curried Cod. The correction states that 'one tablespoonful' of curry powder should read 'one small teaspoonful' of curry powder; an error clearly well worth correcting. Isabella published two more cookery books before dying four years later, after giving birth to her fourth child, when she was just twenty-eight.

With *Household Management* to hand, I'm thinking of preparing Hessian Soup followed by Cod's Head and Shoulders with Pickled Nasturtiums and Canary Pudding. However, I might fall back on Collared Pig's Face with Boiled Salad if I can't face plucking all those canaries.

Chapter 7

ERRONEOUS
EXPLORERS

**Lord Carnarvon, excavator of Tutankhamen's Tomb,
fell prey to the 'Curse of the Pharaohs'**

IN November 1922, amateur
Egyptologist the 5th Earl of
Carnarvon, along with archaeologist Howard Carter, discovered
the tomb of Tutankhamen in
Luxor, Egypt. A few months
later, after excavation had
begun on the tomb, Lord
Carnarvon mysteriously died,
prompting many to claim that
he had fallen victim to the
'Curse of the Pharaohs', which
was alleged to be written on the
wall of the tomb.

One would generally expect a
curse to work instantaneously, but Carnarvon's demise was
rather convoluted. Already frail, the fifty-six-year-old had
been advised to go to Egypt for the good of his health. While
there, he was bitten on the face by a mosquito, and later,

when shaving, he accidentally cut the top off the mosquito bite. This resulted in erysipelas (a bacterial skin infection), followed by blood poisoning, which led to a bout of pneumonia and eventually to his death on 5 April 1923.

T. G. H. James, former Keeper of Egyptian Antiquities at the British Museum and author of *Howard Carter*, explains that 'the death of Lord Carnarvon provided the initial tragedy which established the idea of a baleful influence.' Regarding the age of death of others connected with the find, James reveals that Alan Gardiner died at the age of eighty-four, James Henry Breasted at seventy, Evelyn Herbert at seventy-nine, Harry Burton at sixty-one and Alfred Lucas died aged seventy-eight. Carter, the principal archaeologist, survived sixteen years after the tomb was opened, and passed away peacefully at sixty-six years of age. No one present at the tomb's opening appears to have died particularly prematurely or under unusual circumstances.

Mark R. Nelson's 2002 study, 'The mummy's curse: historical cohort study', published in the *British Medical Journal,* examined the 'survival of individuals exposed to the "mummy's curse"' by following up the fates of forty-four Westerners identified by Howard Carter (pictured left in the image opposite) as present in Egypt at the specified dates, twenty-five of whom were potentially exposed to the curse. Nelson found that 'the mean age at death was seventy years.' From this, he concluded that there was 'no evidence to support the existence of a mummy's curse.'

As for the existence of the curse itself, in a biography of journalist and Egyptologist Arthur Weigall (who was present at the excavation), his granddaughter Julie Hankey reveals that 'Weigall, in common with every other Egyptologist, denied that there was a curse written on the walls of Tutankhamen's tomb.' She explains that when the tomb was opened Carnarvon commented on the number of chairs inside and joked about 'giving a concert in the tomb'. This light-heartedness may have offended Weigall's ethical sensibilities, since he commented 'If he goes down in that spirit, I give him six weeks to live.' Hankey explains that her grandfather passed off the comment as 'one of those prophetic utterances which seem to issue, without a definite intention, from the subconscious brain.' Indeed, Weigall appeared not to mind that the story of the curse of Tutankhamen 'got about', and is even quoted as saying 'See how the public will lap it up.' T. G. H. James is in complete agreement, therefore, when he suggests that 'the origin of the curse may have been due to a casual remark made by Arthur Weigall.'

Perhaps the final word should go to Howard Carter. James quotes him saying that he was 'entirely opposed to the foolish superstitions which are far too prevalent among emotional people in search of "psychic" excitement . . . So far as the living are concerned, curses of this nature have no part in the Egyptian Ritual.'

Now that's been straightened out, who's for that concert in Tutankhamen's tomb?

Sir Walter Raleigh brought back tobacco and the potato from the New World

IT seems that tobacco was doing the rounds in Europe several years before the birth of sixteenth-century adventurer Sir Walter Raleigh (*c.*1552–1618). In *The Oxford Companion to the Body,* Alan W. Cuthbert reveals that as far back as 1492, New World explorer Christopher Columbus was given 'dried fragrant leaves, but threw them away, not realizing the value'. He suggests that Rodrigo de Jerez was 'the first European smoker, learning of the practice from Cubans in the 1490s and taking the habit back to Spain'. The Holy Inquisitors were mightily suspicious of this new activity and Jerez 'was imprisoned . . . for seven years'. By the time he was released, though, everyone was at it.

According to writer Ferdnand Braudel, in 1561 Jean Nicot, French ambassador to Portugal, sent powdered tobacco to the French Queen, Catherine de Medici, 'as a remedy for migraine'. Jordan Goodman reveals in *Tobacco in History* that the plant was called 'nicotiane' in Nicot's honour.

Tobacco did originate from the New World and was grown in what became known as Virginia. However, the *Oxford Dictionary of National Biography* (*DNB*) explains that 'Raleigh himself never went to Virginia.' Though he was keen to explore the New World, his status as a favourite of Queen Elizabeth I meant that she 'would not allow Raleigh to risk such hazardous voyages himself'. In 1573, naval explorers Sir John Hawkins and Sir Francis Drake (who *were* allowed to go to the New World) brought tobacco to England. Cuthbert reveals that Drake 'introduced tobacco to Sir Walter Raleigh in 1585'. The *DNB* reports that

Raleigh then became 'convinced that tobacco was a good cure for coughs'. Biographer John Aubrey explains how Raleigh, while sheltering 'in a Stand at Sir Robert Poyntz parke at Acton ... tooke a pipe of Tobacco, which made the Ladies quitt it till he had donne'.

The misattribution seems to be the fault of academic Henry Buttes, who, when writing about the origins of tobacco in his 1599 book *Dyets Dry Dinner,* stated that 'Syr Walter Rawleigh . . . hath both farre fetcht it, and deare bought it.' Queen Elizabeth's successor, King James I, who found Raleigh considerably less attractive than she had, hated smoking, and since the weed had arrived as a result of New World conquests, he blamed Raleigh. The King, in his 1604 tract *A Counterblaste to Tobacco,* complains that 'it seemes a miracle to me, how a custome springing from so vile a ground, and brought in by a father [Raleigh] so generally hated, should be welcomed upon so slender warrant.' Aubrey consequentially states that 'Sir Walter was the first that brought tobacco into England and into fashion.' Though he was right on the second count but wrong on the first, the erroneous belief persists to this day.

As for the assumption that Raleigh brought the potato back from the New World, this too is a fallacy. An entry in the *DNB* reveals that John Gerard, in his 1597 work *Herball,* appears to have initiated the misapprehension concerning the origin of the vegetable by documenting that he had 'received roots of the potato from Virginia, which grew in his garden'. However, as Alan Romans points out in *The Potato Book*, unlike tobacco 'potatoes did not grow in North America.' In *Science in the British Colonies of America,* Raymond Phineas Stearns claims that Gerard's 'potato' was 'a sweet potato or, possibly, Jerusalem artichoke'.

Romans reveals that Drake *was* given potatoes in Chile, South America in 1577, 'but these could not have survived until his return in 1580.' (Although, doubtless, some present-day supermarkets would estimate they still had a good few weeks' shelf life left.) The *DNB* suggests that the potato originated in Peru, while *The Oxford Companion to Food* explains that Europeans first encountered the potato in 1537, in what is modern-day Colombia. The potato, much as one would expect, crept into Europe by the back door, arriving in Seville by at least 1570 and in Britain during the 1590s, when 'there was no reason at the time for anyone to have paid attention to the introduction of the potato.'

It wasn't an instant success. The *Companion to Food* reveals that 'Protestants would not plant it' since it was 'not mentioned in the Bible'. However, the Catholics got round this tricky issue by 'sprinkling their seed potatoes with holy water and planting them on Good Friday'.

Scottish explorer Dr Livingstone got lost in the Congo

IN the popular imagination, Scottish missionary Dr David Livingstone has gained the reputation of being a rather feckless explorer, since many people believe that he got himself lost in darkest Africa for several years.

After visiting Africa as a missionary in 1841, Livingstone grew determined to explore the region. In an 1853 letter to fellow missionary Robert Moffat, he announced, 'I shall open up a path into the interior, or perish.' In 1858, Livingstone set out on his Zambezi expedition, discovered Victoria Falls, named them after the Queen, then became a national hero and bestselling author. In 1866, he set off on his final exploration to find the source of the Nile. Two years passed and nothing was heard from the popular adventurer.

James Gordon Bennett (*the* Gordon Bennett whose name obligingly stood in for 'gorblimey' in the late nineteenth century), who was editor of *The New York Herald*, hit upon the idea of sending one of his correspondents to search for Livingstone. Welsh-born, naturalized American Henry Morton Stanley (who was brought up at the St Asaph workhouse in Wales) was given the job. In *How I Found Livingstone*, Stanley recalls Bennett telling him to 'draw whatever sums of money were necessary for the prosecution of the search'. Stanley's book, which was described by Florence Nightingale as 'the very worst book on the very best subject I ever saw in my life', reveals how, two years later in 1871, he tracked Livingstone down in the town of Ujiji, on the shores of Lake Tanganyika some time around 23 October (the exact date is uncertain).

Stanley tells how 'as I advanced slowly towards him I noticed he was pale, that he looked wearied and wan.' He took off his hat and (apparently) said, 'Dr Livingstone, I presume?' (Alan Gallop explains in *Mr Stanley, I Presume?* that these famous words appeared in *The New York Herald* dispatch shortly after the meeting, but he adds that some historians have questioned whether Stanley actually uttered them, since the relevant page in his diary is missing and Livingstone's own recollection of the meeting does not mention them.)

Livingstone replied, '"Yes," . . . with a kind, cordial smile, lifting his cap slightly.' Stanley follows this up with 'I thank God, Doctor, that I have been permitted to see you.' Livingstone replied, 'I feel thankful that I am here to wel-

come you.' Stanley confirms that Livingstone 'was not lost, just performing a marvellously thorough, detailed exploration'. He then informs us that 'conversation began . . . What about? I declare I have forgotten.' (I'm starting to see what Florence Nightingale means.)

D. Robert's contribution to the *Oxford Dictionary of National Biography* reveals that the two men 'travelled together to the north end of Lake Tanganyika and proved that it had no outlet there,' adding that 'they parted on 14 March 1872 at Tabora, on the caravan route.' Despite Stanley's suggestion that Livingstone return home, Roberts explains that the adventurer 'resumed his quest'. Unfortunately, when Stanley returned to Britain with news that he had located Dr Livingstone, his claims were ridiculed. Furthermore, Livingstone never did make it back home, and in 1873 he perished in what is now Zambia.

Not to be deterred, Stanley expanded on his new-found profession of explorer-retriever when, according to *Into Africa* author Martin Dugard, Gordon Bennett then 'sent a second *New York Herald* expedition to Africa', this time to find Sir Samuel White Baker despite the fact that 'Baker wasn't lost and certainly didn't need to be rescued.' In 1887, Stanley led yet a third expedition with the intention of rescuing Emin Pasha from the Sudan.

The *Oxford Companion to American Literature* explains that although Stanley was 'an American citizen . . . he resumed his English citizenship and was knighted in 1899' – presumably for services rendered in the retrieval of lost explorers. Not bad for a former workhouse boy.

Captain Cook was eaten by Hawaiian cannibals

IN 1776, the renowned English naval explorer Captain James Cook set out with his crew on the *Resolution* to discover the western opening of the fabled North-West Passage through Canada. When winter set in, Cook stopped off at the Hawaiian Islands where he made friends with the natives and was worshipped as a god. Not bad, as winter breaks go.

In 1779, Cook left to continue his expedition, but was forced to return for repairs. During his second stay, the Hawaiians stole a sailing boat. When Cook attempted to recover the boat, fighting broke out on the beach at Kealakekua. In *The Trial of the Cannibal Dog*, history professor Anne Salmond explains that during a lull in firing 'one man struck him on the back of the head with a club, while another stabbed him in the neck with one of his own iron trade daggers.'

The saying 'everybody wants a piece of me' was literally true in the case of the venerated Captain Cook. In *The Apotheosis of Captain Cook,* Gananath Obeyeskere quotes ship's surgeon's mate David Samwell revealing that Cook's clothes were then 'sold in the cabin'. His crew requested the return of his body, but Salmond states that Hawaiian priest Keli'ikea then confessed that, much like his belongings, 'Cook's body had been dismembered and . . . divided among the high chiefs.'

Keli'ikea explained that 'his head had been given to Kamehameha, the legs, thighs, arms and lower jaw to Kalani'opu'u, and the rest of his body had been burnt to avenge the breach of the high chief's sacred power.' The

crew, suspecting something more sinister, asked whether Cook's body had, in fact, been eaten. Salmond reports that 'Keli'ikea was aghast' at the suggestion. He reassured the crew that 'his people were not cannibals.' The *Oxford Dictionary of National Biography* agrees that Cook's body was 'according to custom, cut up and the flesh scraped from the bones and ceremonially burnt, the bones being distributed among the various chiefs.' Obeyeskere agrees that 'Cook's body was ritually dismembered, burnt, and distributed among chiefs as if he were an important chief.'

Keli'ikea did his best to recover Cook's remains, which he delivered, as Obeyeskere says, 'very decently wrapped up'. Salmond confirms this, explaining that the crew was given a black feather cloak containing 'bones with burnt flesh attached, which included Cook's thighs and legs, but not his feet'.

The crew recovered 'both arms with the hands separated from them, but joined to the skin of his forearms, and his skull and scalp with one ear attached, although the facial bones were missing'. The hands had been preserved in salt. That afternoon, Salmond reports that Cook's recovered remains were 'buried in the sea with full military honours'.

The noble Captain Cook was indeed cooked by Hawaiian natives but, thankfully, he didn't suffer the ignominy of becoming lunch: rather his remains were destined to become sacred artefacts until the Hawaiian priests realized that it would be more politic to return them for burial at sea by his crew.

Chapter 8

CALUMNIOUS CLAIMS

**In past centuries, witches were ducked
to test their guilt**

IN the seventeenth and eighteenth centuries, 'ducking' consisted of being secured to a wooden seesaw-type construction called a ducking stool and being plunged into a river or pond. This was not a test, but a punishment. In *Crime and Mentalities in Early Modern England*, author Malcolm Gaskill points out that the ducking of scolds and the swimming of witches is often confused. Owen Davies explains in *Witchcraft, Magic and Culture* that ducking

stools were used to punish a variety of minor offences 'such as the wearing of inappropriate dress on feast days, violation of the laws of weights and measures, and scolding.' Henry Fielding's 1739 essay *'Jurgatur Verbis'*, included in *Contributions to the Champion, and Related Writings,* confides that 'a Scold is very often dreaded by her whole Neighbourhood, and I much question whether my Wife's Tongue be not as great a Terror to all her Acquaintance as my Cudgel can be.' He explains that since 'an evil tongue' is 'little less than a Sword in a Madman's Hands . . . [in] certain Districts, they have erected over Canals a wooden Stool, wherein the Offender being plac'd, is to be very severely ducked.' Jane Marshall reveals in *Three Tours of England's Wonderful Abbeys* that the last recorded use of this apparatus in England was at Leominster in 1809, when Jane Curran (also known as Jenny Pipes) 'was ducked in one of the adjacent streams'.

Witches, on the other hand, were 'swum'. A 1613 London pamphlet, *Witches Apprehended, Examined and Executed* contained directions on the continental practice of 'swimming' a witch. The ritual was based on the assumption, as explained in King James I's 1597 witch-hunters handbook *Daemonologie,* that 'God hath appointed . . . that the water shall refuse to receive them in her bosom, that have shaken off them the sacred water of Baptisme.' With hands and feet bound, suspects were thrown into a river or pond. If the water refused them and they floated, they were guilty; if the water accepted them as rightfully baptized, and they sank, they were innocent. For those who could not read, as Davies explains, the pamphlet also contained a woodcut illustration, which 'provided a good pictorial demonstration of the method'.

According to Davies, test case Mary Sutton of Milton, Bedfordshire, on whom the London pamphlet was based, finished up with rather inconclusive results: in her first swimming, she sank; in her second, she floated. She was then tried by a magistrate, found guilty and hanged – rendering the swimming somewhat redundant. Nevertheless, the practice of swimming still caught on.

Scottish clan tartans date back to ancient times

IT's a brave man (or ferret – I'll explain later) who sports a kilt bearing the tartan of a clan from which he is not descended. Scottish clan tartans are thought to date back to antiquity, yet the truth about tartan heritage is rather different and includes a sizeable contribution from two conmen named Allen.

The earliest known representation of Highland dress is John Michael Wright's painting *A Highland Chieftain*, dating to the late seventeenth century. The impressive chieftain is believed to be a Campbell yet, intriguingly, the pattern that he wears bears no resemblance to that of any Campbell tartan or any other established tartan of today. In *A History of the Clan Campbell* (Volume 1) – a very interesting read, even if you aren't a Campbell – Alastair Campbell states that the tartan in the painting is an 'irregular one', which is 'very often the case with early tartans'. In fact, there are very few references to specific tartans in fifteenth- and sixteenth-century writing.

Historically, tartan's distinctive cross-checked repeating pattern known as a 'sett' was loosely associated with regions, not clans. In *Europe: A History*, Norman Davies adds that even this convention was not followed 'by ordinary folk'. Historian Magnus Magnusson points out in *Scotland: The Story of a Nation* that in 1746, at the Battle of Culloden, 'there were no tartans as distinguishing emblems of clan loyalty.' This view is confirmed in David Morier's contemporary painting *The Battle of Culloden*, in which the Jacobites are wearing a variety of differing tartans. Later in the century, *Encyclopaedia Britannica* reveals that portraits 'show the Highland gentleman wearing such tartans as pleased him in colour and design, including different garments of unrelated tartans', which suggests that one's choice of tartan was more a question of taste than an indicator of kinship.

The start of the tartan craze can be dated back to the early nineteenth century when, in 1822, at the invitation of novelist Sir Walter Scott, King George IV paid an official visit to Edinburgh and did much to popularize the trend by wearing a kilt. Beneath the garment, as related in David McCrone's *Understanding Scotland*, the King wore a 'fetching pair of pink tights'. Fortunately, some might say, that particular trend didn't catch on, but it was at this gathering that the custom of linking a sett with a specific clan began to be established.

This task was later aided, Norman Davies reveals, by 'two charlatan brothers, the self-styled Sobieski Stuarts'. These men were, in reality, John and Charles Allen, who claimed to be long-lost Polish/Jacobite royalty. They produced what Davies describes as a 'finely illustrated, but spurious work' grandly titled the *Vestiarium Scoticum (Scottish Dress)*. They claimed that the tome was a copy of a sixteenth-century work belonging to the Bishop of Ross. In an 1842 advert, printed in a booklet entitled *Observations on Extension of Protection of Copyright of Designs,* John Sobieski Stuart announced that the work had been 'splendidly got up, at a great expense . . . 45 copies for Sale . . . Ten Guineas each'. As Magnusson explains, the book 'purported to describe the authentic ancient clan tartans of Scotland'.

Describing it as a 'splendid work of fiction', Alastair Campbell cites a letter to J. F. Campbell of Islay from Sobieski Stuart, stating that the 6th Duke of Argyll generally wore the 42nd [the blue, black and green tartan commonly known as Black Watch after the Highland regiment] until, in 1824, he 'adopted the bright sprainges' [yellow and white striped tartan] which previously he'd had 'no knowledge of . . . until I told him of the tradition'. It was in 1819, apparently, that the said tradition had been confided to Sobieski Stuart by a 'very old Campbell woman on Loch Awe side'. 'The bright stripes were for the chief and his house only.' Campbell suspects that 'the tartan with the yellow and white stripe, so beloved by successive experts on the subject of tartan, is no more than fabrication by the ingenious brothers, who were the source of so many of today's "Clan" tartans.' (Nowadays, Campbell explains that his clansfolk are advised to avoid the so-called Campbell of Argyll or Campbell of Lochawe tartan 'if they wish to be correct'.)

Campbell also points out that on occasions, the Sobieski brothers produced 'a different sett for a Clan who thought they already had one'. In *Clans & Tartans*, James MacKay adds that 'ironically, many of the tartans invented by the Sobieski Stuarts . . . now rank among the oldest, and therefore most authentic patterns.' Davies concludes that the allocation of tartans to specific clan names 'completed a remarkable process of cultural invention, which had been evolving over two centuries.'

In modern times, the right to use certain plaid patterns is still jealously guarded. On 12 October 2005, *The Daily Telegraph* reported that the fashion house Burberry threatened to sue the owner of a ferret accessory shop for supplying unauthorized ferret-wear in the famous Burberry check. When quizzed on whether Burberry was planning its own ferret accessory range, a spokesman was reported as stating that there were no plans for a Burberry ferret line at that time, but 'that's not to say there won't be.' Watch this space . . .

The Olympic Games have been staged regularly since the days of Ancient Greece

THE original festival was held in Olympia, Greece from 776 BCE and featured athletic, literary and musical competitions every four years. In *The Building Program of Herod the Great*, Duane W. Roller reveals that in 12 BCE, King Herod championed the impoverished event and became lifetime president. (So he wasn't all bad.)

In fact, the *Oxford Dictionary of Phrase and Fable* reveals that the Games were 'abolished by the Roman Emperor Theodosius' in 393 CE because of the festival's pagan associations. It wasn't until the early nineteenth century that calls were made for the Games to be re-established, when, in 1833, Greek poet Panagiotis Soutsos called for the return of the Games in his poem 'Dialogues of the Dead'. An entry in the *Oxford Dictionary of National Biography* reveals that in 1850, English doctor William Penny Brookes set up the Wenlock Olympian Society in Wenlock, Shropshire, which resulted in the staging of annual games 'for literary and fine-art attainments, and for skill and strength in athletic exercise.' Similar to the original Olympics, the event was open to those whom Brookes termed as 'every grade of man'. In 1859, wealthy Greek businessman Evangelis Zappas financed a revival of the Games in Athens. A couple of years later, inspired by Zappas's success, Brookes established the Shropshire Olympian Games, and in 1865, helped found the National

Olympian Society in the UK. These first games were held at Crystal Palace in the following year and attracted over 10,000 spectators. Brookes's international efforts, however, floundered until Frenchman Baron Pierre de Coubertin took up what he described as 'the splendid and beneficent task' and succeeded in establishing a permanent international event. So, in 1896, the first modern Olympic Games were staged at a new stadium in Athens, in which twelve countries competed.

In the opening ceremony of the modern Olympics, a relay runner carries the flame, originating from the Temple of Hera, to light the torch in the host city with the implication that the Olympic flame has been continuously burning in the temple for 3,000 years. Quite how anybody could still be taken in by such a suggestion is baffling. *Encyclopaedia Britannica* reveals that 'contrary to popular belief, the torch relay from the Temple of Hera in Olympia to the host city has no predecessor or parallel in antiquity.' The original Games were held in Olympia, so there was no need to run the torch anywhere. *Britannica* adds that the Olympic flame 'first appeared at the 1928 Olympics in Amsterdam'. The torch relay was thought up by Carl Diem, organizer of the 1936 Berlin Games, where it 'made its debut'. The original Olympians competed naked. This tradition, however, was not carried over to today's competitions. After all, let's not forget that modern competitors need somewhere to pin their numbers.

In 1795, German came within one vote of replacing English as America's official language

AFTER the American Revolution, the newly formed United States was keen to establish its hard-won independence from Britain. In a 1797 letter to the Princess Royal, eighteenth-century British etymologist Sir Herbert Croft claimed that Americans had considered 'revenging themselves on England, by rejecting its language and adopting that of France'. *We'll show the British! We'll become fluent in French and see how they like that!* It's easy to see how throwing tea into the harbour found more favour with dissidents.

The modern version of this legend is that, after the Revolution, America's official language was not to be French, but German. There is a grain of truth residing at the heart of this claim, but not a very big one. In *Linguistic Culture and Language Policy*, language professor Harold F. Schiffman explains how, in 1794, the German-speaking citizens of Virginia, quite reasonably, petitioned the Third Congress 'to print some copies of federal laws in German'. Congress debated the matter several times and came to a vote in January 1795. The speaker of the house, one Frederick August Muhlenberg of Pennsylvania, had been one of the original sponsors of the proposal. To avoid prejudicing the vote, he stood down as Speaker. *Progress in Language Planning* describes how, as a result, the vote was 'rejected by forty-two votes to forty-one'.

The refusal to print statutes in German for the edification of German speakers grew into the myth that the German language was narrowly defeated when nominated to be the official language of America. Indeed, Schiffman adds that there followed more requests for laws to be printed in German, but they all failed 'on the grounds that English was already the official language of the republic'.

In *A History of the English Language*, Richard M. Hogg explains that unlike countries such as France, Greece and Chile, America in common with Great Britain 'has no official language' although English is considered the national language in both countries.

Alexander Fleming twice saved Winston Churchill's life

THIS tale, often featured in inspirational works and self-help volumes, dates back to the 1950s. It tells of how a Scottish farmer's son 'Alex' Fleming saves a young Winston Churchill from drowning in a Scottish lake. Churchill's father arrives in a fine carriage at the farmer's house, full of gratitude, and funds the impoverished 'Alex' Fleming's medical education. (Incidentally, Fleming was known by the diminutive 'Alec' rather than 'Alex'.) During the course of his work Fleming discovers penicillin, which, years later, then saves the life of, you guessed it, an ailing Winston Churchill. The Churchill Centre describes this tale as 'certainly a fiction' for several reasons.

Winston Churchill lived in Ireland as a small child, but not Scotland. On his return to London, he attended boarding school from the age of eight. If Churchill had met with such an accident, his parents would not have been likely to notice. Janice Hamilton's biographical work *Winston Churchill* records that the lad didn't have much contact with his parents, who, although professing fondness for him, often neglected to visit him, even when they were passing his boarding school.

As for the penicillin connection, in 1944, Churchill did contract pneumonia. It was suggested that he be treated with the new drug penicillin, but according to Walter Gratzer, author of *Eurekas and Euphorias*, it was the more traditional drug sulphonamide that was administered, which resulted in Churchill's recovery. Rumours of a penicillin cure, however, persisted. In *Alexander Fleming*, Gwyn Macfarlane claims that 'the tale of the rescue from drowning is particularly absurd since Churchill was seven years older than Fleming.' The Churchill Centre reveals that the story apparently originated in a 1950s book *Worship Programs for Juniors*. The tale was included in a chapter entitled 'The Power of Kindness,' the lesson presumably being: *saving a drowning child isn't just a moral obligation – there can be something in it for you, too.*

Chapter 9

COUNTERFEIT KINGS
(POST-CONQUEST)

Robert the Bruce was inspired to defeat the English after watching a spider spin a web

THE Norman Bruce family was related by marriage to the Scottish royal family and arrived in Scotland in the early twelfth century. In 1290, the Scottish throne became vacant and the sixth Robert the Bruce claimed it. However, the English king Edward I declared feudal superiority over the Scots and awarded the crown to John de Balliol. The eighth Robert the Bruce eventually gained the Scottish throne in 1306. He ousted the English from Scotland at the Battle of Bannockburn in 1314 and ultimately won Scottish independence in the Treaty of Northampton in 1328.

The story goes that while Robert the Bruce hid out on Rathlin Island off the coast of Northern Ireland (the location is sometimes cited as Jura Island in the Inner Hebrides of Scotland), he was inspired to persevere in battling the English by watching a spider making repeated attempts to spin its web. However, Robert Gambles points out in

Breaking Butterflies that 'no mention is made of the famous incident in John Barbour's fourteenth-century poem "The Bruce".' In the preface of a 1997 reprint of the work, A. A. M. Duncan agrees that 'there is no authority for it earlier than the eighteenth century.' He explains that 'it is a folk tale . . . borrowed for Bruce because he did indeed try and try again.'

It would appear that nineteenth-century Scottish writer Sir Walter Scott was the individual responsible for popularizing the misattribution. In his 1829–30 work *Tales of a Grandfather: History of Scotland,* he writes that while Bruce was staying in 'a miserable dwelling at Rachrin [Rathlin Island]', an incident took place which, 'although it rests only on tradition in families of the name of Bruce, is rendered probable by the manners of the time.' According to Scott, Bruce was lying 'on his wretched bed [when] . . . his eye was attracted by a spider'. Scott explains how the spider made six unsuccessful attempts to 'swing itself from one beam in the roof to another', and then describes how Bruce had 'fought just six

battles against the English and their allies, and that the poor persevering spider was exactly in the same situation with himself'. Bruce decided to be 'guided by the luck which shall attend this spider'. The spider succeeded and so Bruce went on to have another bash at the English. Scott assures us that 'I have often met with people of the name of Bruce, so completely persuaded of the truth of the story, that they will not on any account kill a spider.'

Magnus Magnusson suggests in *Scotland* that the tale 'first appeared two hundred years earlier in a history of the Douglas family', written by historian and poet David Hume. Interestingly, in his seventeenth-century work *History of the House and Race of Douglas and Angus,* Hume claims that it wasn't Bruce who saw the spider, but Bruce's captain, James Douglas, who was known as 'Black Douglas' to the English and 'Good Sir James' to the Scots. The spider in question was building its web in a tree and it made twelve attempts before succeeding. Douglas, having observed this, advised Bruce to 'follow the example of the spider, to poush forward your Majestie's fortune once more, and hazard yet our persones the 13 tyme.' Thus, in true Hollywood fashion, the best lines were attributed to Bruce the triumphant hero, even though it was Douglas, his trusty ally, who is believed to have said them originally.

King Richard III was a hunchback

THE image most associated with King Richard III is that of Sir Laurence Olivier lolloping about like Quasimodo in the 1955 film. Of course, this is William Shakespeare's interpretation of the fifteenth-century monarch: 'deformed, unfinished, sent before my time / Into this breathing world, scarce half made up.' King Richard's portrait in the Royal Collection, thought to have been painted around 1520 (thirty-five years after Richard's death), appears to corroborate this image, as it features the King with his right shoulder markedly raised. However, in the *Encyclopedia of the Middle Ages*, W. Mark Ormrod states that 'there is no evidence to support the tradition, popularized by Shakespeare, that he was a hunchback.'

Shakespeare was merely dramatizing the words of Sir Thomas More (later Chancellor of England), who, in his

1518 work *History of King Richard III*, describes Richard as 'little of stature, ill-featured of limbs, crookbacked, his left shoulder much higher than his right, hard-favoured of visage.' More adds that he was 'malicious, wrathful, envious' and had the temerity to be a breech birth coming 'into the world feet forward . . . and also not untoothed [with teeth].' In *Breaking Butterflies*, Robert Gambles suggests that More based his work on Civic Records of 1491 found in the archives of the City of York, in which one John Payntour accuses Richard of being 'an hypocrite, a crookback and buried in a ditch like a dog'. (An entry by Rosemary Horrox in the *Oxford Dictionary of National Biography* claims that after his death at Bosworth Field, Richard was buried in the church of the Franciscans at Leicester.)

In *History of the Kings of England,* fifteenth-century priest and antiquary John Rous suggests that Richard was 'small of stature, with a short face and unequal shoulders, the right higher and the left lower'. (The opposite shoulder is cited by More.) Rous also makes the unlikely claim that Richard was 'retained within his mother's womb for two years, emerging with teeth and hair to his shoulders'. However, the associated line drawing of Richard and Queen Anne Neville featured in the Rous Roll (a family chronicle of the Earls of Warwick compiled on a roll of parchment by John Rous) depicts a delightful couple. A benign-looking, even-shouldered Richard raises a sword, sceptre-like, in his right hand. (Anne looks startled, but that seems to be because her eyebrows have been drawn on too high.)

In his 1534 book *English History*, Polydore Vergil writes that Richard was 'little of stature, [and] deformyd of body' but he downgrades Richard's 'crookback' to no more than a 'throne showlder being higher than thother' although, suspiciously, he doesn't say which one. Horrox points out that 'contemporary chroniclers seem to agree that Richard was small and slight, and the Crowland chronicler refers to his haggard face . . . [and] if Richard did have some physical deformity it is likely to have been slight, probably no more than . . . uneven shoulders.' Philip Rhodes's 1977 research paper 'The Physical Deformity of Richard III', suggests that Richard 'showed a normal though unusual raised shoulder'. Possibly, due to his slight stature, he may have employed 'vigorous exercises, especially [sword] fighting' that may have resulted in overdeveloped right shoulder muscles or he may have had 'a minor degree of Sprengel's deformity [inherited elevated shoulder blade]'.

A *Dictionary of British History* suggests that 'the supposed peculiarities of his birth and the hunchback . . . were . . . inventions to signify evil.' This would appear to be the case, since Alison Weir points out in *The Princes in the Tower* that the hunchbacked portrait in the Royal Collection was doctored: 'X-rays taken in the 1950s and 1973 show that the right shoulder has been overpainted above the still-visible original shoulder line by a later hand, and that the eyes have been narrowed.' Subsequent monarchs were descended not from Richard III, but from Henry Tudor, who seized Richard's throne on his death in 1485 and became Henry VII. It's not surprising, therefore, that after Richard's demise, Tudor statesmen such as More and Rous took care to portray Richard III in a damning light. *Encyclopaedia Britannica* adds that 'Modern scholars . . . tend to regard him as a potentially capable monarch whose reputation for wickedness originated in sixteenth-century political propaganda.' Nowadays Richard has a whole society dedicated to clearing his name.

Henry VIII had six wives

DURING his reign (1509–47), Tudor king Henry VIII found himself saddled with a succession of unsatisfactory queens, which caused him one big problem: how was he to extricate himself from the marriages when, as a good Catholic, he deeply disapproved of divorce? Coupled with this, the Roman Catholic church did not recognize the unholy practice. The answer lay in annulment.

Thus, *The Oxford Companion to British History* reveals that 'Henry VIII was technically never divorced – his marriages to Catherine of Aragon and Anne of Cleves were annulled.' In *Dissolving Wedlock*, Colin S. Gibson confirms that 'Henry never divorced a wife' and adds to the list of annulments by stating that 'he annulled his marriages to Catherine of Aragon, Anne Boleyn and Anne of Cleves.' Annulments also had the advantage of being regarded as more 'valid' than divorce. Roderick Phillips points out in *Untying the Knot* that 'Henry's insistence on pursuing the annulments suggests that he himself, despite his popular

image, was more fastidious in matrimonial matters than he is normally given credit for.' Technically, three of Henry VIII's marriages never officially existed, he never divorced and was merely twice bereaved.

Catherine of Aragon, Henry's first wife, was previously married to his elder brother Arthur, who died a year later. With Henry she gave birth to six children (including two sons), but only Mary survived infancy. For this reason, as the *Collins Dictionary of British History* explains, he sought from Pope Clement VII an annulment of his twenty-year marriage to Catherine, but the Pope refused. One reason suggested as a cause for this course of action was that he felt he had committed incest with his brother's wife, and he therefore went ahead with the annulment without the Pope's consent. This momentous act led to the historic break with the Roman Catholic Church. Henry created the Church of England with himself as Supreme Head, which set England on the often rocky path of Protestantism.

Not long into Henry's next 'marriage' to the feisty but deeply unpopular Anne Boleyn, Henry's advisers 'discovered' that Anne had been previously engaged to someone else, and thus their marriage was annulled in 1536. Just for good measure, Henry had Anne's head sliced off for allegedly committing adultery during the time when she hadn't even been legally married to him. (The King had clearly bagsied all the lawyers.)

Henry immediately married Jane Seymour, who had the good sense to quit while she was still in favour and who died twelve days after giving birth to the much-longed-for, future king, Edward VI. His disastrous fourth marriage to Anne of Cleves was, Phillips reveals, 'also annulled'. This annulment was the only one with any modern validity, since 'her physical appearance was such as to have rendered him [the King] impotent.' Non-consummation is still valid grounds for annulment of a marriage today.

Nineteen days later, Henry appeared to have recovered his faculties since he then married Anne's maid of honour, the flighty eighteen-year-old Catherine Howard. In less

than two years, however, Catherine was charged with treason for committing adultery. She had also been engaged prior to her marriage but insisted she hadn't been, so with no grounds for annulment and guilty of treason, Henry obviously had no choice but to behead her.

Parliament then passed a bill declaring it treason for an unchaste woman to marry the King. It breathed a collective sigh of relief when Henry married thirty-one-year-old Catherine Parr in 1543. Since she was twice widowed, she couldn't reasonably be expected to be a virgin. Catherine would also survive Henry, who died four years later aged fifty-two, before going on to marry a fourth time.

Thus, the famous mnemonic designed to help students recall the fates of Henry's wives – divorced, beheaded, died, divorced, beheaded, survived – should more correctly read: annulled, beheaded (and annulled), died, annulled, beheaded, survived.

The distinction between divorce and annulment is important because Henry's refusal to consider divorce set the pattern for the following 300 years. Phillips points out that 'although a limited form of divorce was established in the eighteenth century, it was not until the mid nineteenth century that a divorce law was passed in England.'

The boy-king Edward VI was sickly from birth

EDWARD VI, Henry VIII's only legitimate son, came to the throne on his father's death in 1547 at the age of nine. He reigned for six years before succumbing to what was probably tuberculosis. Though he is famous for being sickly, D. M. Loades writes in *John Dudley* that 'he was not the pale, sickly child of romantic imagination, but a thoroughly healthy and normal boy.'

It's difficult to judge the athletic prowess of a newborn, but according to Antonia Fraser in *The Six Wives of Henry VIII*, Lord Chancellor Thomas Cromwell attempted it by informing the French ambassador that the Prince was 'in good health' and 'sucketh like a child of his puissance [standing]'. Similarly, Christopher Morris reveals in *The Tudors* that Edward 'was not weedy . . . nor did he, until his final illness (which lasted only seven months), lack robustness.' Indeed, Hans Holbein's portrait of baby Edward depicts a fabulously chubby-faced child. In *The Last Tudor*

King, Hester Chapman describes how one doctor confided to the French ambassador that Edward was 'so fat, unhealthy and over-fed that he cannot live long'.

Though Edward was believed to have caught malaria at Hampton Court when he was only four years old, Chapman reveals how 'doctors told Henry that Edward's inherent strength would probably save him,' which it did. A year later the French ambassador was describing the five-year-old as 'handsome, strong and marvellously big for his age'. An entry in the *Oxford Dictionary of National Biography* reveals how 'when left to himself, he matched the swordplay, jousting, and riding with long hours in self-absorbed study of fortifications and war.' While in Katharine MacDonogh's *Reigning Cats and Dogs*, Edward

is alleged to have once torn a live falcon into four pieces in a fit of rage, which suggests his constitution was far from weak or sickly.

With the Protestant Edward's Catholic half-sister Mary waiting in the wings, sympathetic foreign ambassadors may have been responsible for starting up rumours regarding his apparent ill health. A month after

Edward's birth, Chapman reveals that the French ambassador 'was writing jubilantly that Edward was dead'. Two years later he was being described as 'slightly ill', and three years later he had a 'weak constitution'. Later still Edward had 'a natural weakness' and news was sent to France that he could not possibly live much longer. However, according to Chapman, after his bout of malaria Edward did not have 'a day's illness' until April 1552. It was at this time that Edward fell ill with something akin to measles and smallpox, which by Christmas 1552 had developed into the early stages of tuberculosis.

Morris reveals that by 1553 Edward was reported as having 'a tough, strong, straining cough . . . the sputum [of which] . . . smells beyond measure.' In July 1553, he died in his sixteenth year, which paved the way for Queen Mary and the revival of Catholicism.

After Queen Anne, King George I was next in line to the British throne

MANY regard inheriting a throne as a blood right. Yet, in 1714 there were around fifty applicants with a stronger blood claim to the British throne than King George I, but they were all passed over because they were the wrong religion. George I was of royal blood, but it was rather watered down when compared to the numerous Catholic claimants who were more closely related to the late Queen Anne than George.

In 1714, Queen Anne (whose father was the Catholic Stuart James II) died. Her nearest living relative was her exiled Catholic half-brother James Edward, known as the Old Pretender, since he was 'pretending' – with some justification – that he had a right to succeed to his half-sister's throne. As early as 1701, French king Louis XIV proclaimed James King of England. However, as Brenda Ralph Lewis reveals in *Monarchy*, 'the Protestant

Parliament would have none of that.' *Encyclopaedia Britannica* agrees that 'James's adherence to Roman Catholicism caused the English Parliament to pass a bill of attainder against him.' The *Oxford Dictionary of National Biography* explains the successor to the British throne 'had to be a Protestant . . . and of Stuart descent, a combination that automatically excluded over fifty claimants with a closer hereditary claim.' So it was that numerous relatives were passed over before they tracked down the nearest Protestant heir, who happened to be the elderly Sophia, Electress of Hanover. A granddaughter of James I of England (known as James VI in Scotland), Sophia was actually fifty-second in line to the throne.

As the Electress of Hanover died just before Queen Anne, so Sophia's son, fifty-four-year-old George Louis of Brunswick-Lüneburg in Lower Saxony (Germany) was shipped in to rule over his new kingdom. George I never really felt settled in England. He became famous for speaking no English and, according to Dr J. H. Plumb in *The First Four Georges*, for imprisoning his estranged wife, Sophia Dorothea of Celle, in Ahlden Castle, Saxony (for the crime of adultery), where she remained until her death 'thirty-two years later'.

George I inherited the British throne in a rather unconventional fashion: he didn't leave a great historical legacy, but religious continuity of the monarch was maintained and this no doubt aided national stability.

Chapter 10

MUDDLED
MILITARIA

'Yankee Doodle' originated as an American Revolutionary song

THE 'Yankee Doodle' air, characteristic of United States nationalism, dates back to before the American Revolutionary War of 1775. *The Oxford Essential Dictionary of the US Military* reveals that 'the lyrics are of British origin', and were set to what was probably a folk tune or marching tune of the time.

The *Concise Oxford Dictionary of Music* claims that the 'earliest printed version of the tune under this title 'appeared in *Aird's Selection of Scotch, English, Irish, and Foreign Airs for the Fife, Violin, or German Flute* (Volume I) published in Glasgow around 1775'. The *Dictionary of the US Military* also reveals that the song was 'composed in the 1750s, during the French and Indian War' (also known as the Seven Years War – 1756–63). During this war, British and colonial forces fought side by side to fend off French domination of America. The precise origin of the lyrics remains uncertain, but the *Oxford English Dictionary* (*OED*) states that the tune is 'said to have been composed in 1755 by Dr Shuckburgh'. The *Oxford Companion to American*

Literature agrees that 'it has often been attributed to a Dr Shuckburgh, a British army surgeon.' The *OED* records that the lyrics were originally 'in derision of the provincial troops' with whom the British soldiers were serving.

It's not clear from where the term 'Yankee' derives, but the *OED* suggests that the 'most plausible conjecture' is that it comes from the Dutch *Janke*, which is short for Jan [John], and suggests that it was 'applied as a derisive nickname by either Dutch or English in the New England states'. 'Doodle', the *OED* reveals, originated in the seventeenth century and was an English term for 'a silly or foolish fellow'.

Yankee Doodle, you will recall from the song, 'stuck a feather in his cap / And called it Macaroni', which is puzzling, since macaroni is a hollow pasta tube that doesn't resemble a feather in the slightest. The *OED* explains that the reference is to the eighteenth-century London Macaroni Club, which was originally set up when macaroni was an exotic foreign delicacy to 'indicate the preference of the members for foreign cookery'. Members of the Macaroni Club were young men well known for travelling through Europe where they 'extravagantly imitated Continental tastes and fashions'. In other words, the British troops were ribbing their colonial counterparts for not being as debonair as they liked to believe, which is a reasonably mild jibe as soldier humour goes.

Twelve years later, during the Revolutionary War, these very colonials were fighting the British. According to Reverend William Gordon of Roxbury, America, in his 1788 work *The History of the Rise, Progress, and Establishment, of the Independence of the United States* (Volume I), before the Battle of Lexington, British troops 'under Lord Percy marched out playing, by way of contempt, "Yankee Doodle", a song composed in derision of the New Englanders, scornfully called *Yankees*'.

When the tide turned in favour of the colonial troops, they sung the song back at the British troops. In 1775, the *OED* cites the *Pennsylvania Evening Post* reporting that British General Gage's troops 'are much dispirited . . . and . . . disposed to leave off dancing any more to the tune of "Yankey Doodle" [sic]'. However, this did not stop the people of America wholeheartedly adopting the song and making it their own.

The Nazi swastika is an ancient symbol for bad luck

THE swastika comprises an equilateral cross with its arms bent at right angles, in the same rotary direction, going clockwise. The *Oxford Dictionary of World History* explains that the word derives from the Sanskrit *svastika* meaning 'conducive to well-being'. The left-handed or anticlockwise swastika, the *sauvastika*, is sometimes, although not always, associated with bad luck. In some designs, it simply features as a mirror image of the swastika.

Swastikas can be found on Roman mosaics and, more recently, were incorporated into the floor design of thirteenth-century Amiens Cathedral in France. In fact, the symbol has been discovered among the relics of primitive people all over the world, including the Ancient Greeks and the Aztecs. In 1908, in Northern Ontario, Canada, a small community founded around a mining site was (and still is) named Swastika. In *A Concise Companion to the Jewish Religion*, Louis Jacobs states that 'archaeological discoveries of swastikas on ancient synagogues show that these were used by Jews, too, albeit only as decorations.' In the 1900s, many nations recognized the swastika as a good-luck symbol.

Encyclopaedia Britannica reveals that 'in Nazi Germany the swastika, with its oblique arms turned clockwise, became the national symbol.' It was adopted because, as *The Oxford Companion to World War II* points out, the swastika 'was thought, incorrectly, to be Teutonic in origin'.

In his 1927 political manifesto *Mein Kampf* (*My Struggle*) – referred to by party critics of the times as *Mein Krampf* (*My Cramp*) – Adolf Hitler devotes several paragraphs to explaining how he personally came up with the design. He confides that 'I, as [party] leader, was unwilling to make public my own design, as it was possible that someone else could come forward with a design just as good, if not better, than my own.' (You have to watch out for that type of thing if you're the prospective Führer.) He explains that he had to discard 'innumerable suggestions . . . among which were many that had incorporated the swastika'. Hitler then concedes that 'a dental surgeon from Starnberg submitted a good design very similar to mine, with only one mistake, in that his swastika . . . was set upon a white background'. The resultant red flag had 'a white disc bearing in its centre a black swastika'. Hitler takes pains to add that he 'also designed' the Nazi Party standard. Of course he did.

The belief that Hitler chose the supposed bad-luck symbol of the sauvastika instead of or even in preference to the swastika, stems from confusion in the definition of 'left-hand' and 'right-hand' swastikas. All authorities agree that right-hand swastikas symbolize good luck. The majority, including *Britannica,* describe the right-hand swastika as having its legs pointing *to* the right. However, a tiny minority (e.g. Rudiger Dahlke's art book *Mandalas of the World*) describe this as a left-handed swastika since, were it jet-propelled (imagine exhaust flames emitting from its legs), it would rotate *to* the left.

In the grand scheme of things, it seems an odd point to dispute. There abound far better examples of Hitler's shortcomings than the possibility that he got his flag symbol back to front.

The number of hooves raised on equestrian statues reveals how the rider died

I F the horse has all four legs on the ground, the rider survived battle unwounded. If the horse has two legs on the ground, the rider died in battle, and if the horse has three legs on the ground, the rider was wounded in battle and died from his wounds. This so-called code for determining how the subject of an equestrian statue died is particularly popular with schoolchildren.

Thomas Thornycroft's 1869 equestrian statue of Queen Victoria in St George's Plateau, Lime Street, Liverpool has one hoof raised. As even the most inattentive of schoolchildren knows, Queen Victoria was never wounded in battle, so it clearly doesn't work in all cases. The claim is quickly disproved by studying the statues of someone who saw a bit more military service than her late Majesty: namely the Duke of Wellington.

Glasgow's statue of the Duke (complete with traditional traffic-cone headgear) has all four hooves firmly rooted to the ground. A second statue of the Duke in Aldershot also has all four of his horse's hooves on the ground. So far, so good: the Duke died in his bed at the age of eighty-three.

However, Sir John Steel's bronze statue of Wellington sited in Princes Street, Edinburgh (known as the Iron Duke, in bronze by Steel) depicts his horse with two hooves raised, implying that he died in battle, which of course he didn't.

Neither does it work for equestrian statues of US General George Washington. Henry Mervin Shrady's statue at Valley Forge, Brooklyn, New York shows Washington's horse with all four hooves on the ground, indicating that he died peacefully in his bed, which, like Wellington, he did aged sixty-seven. Yet the statue at Union Square Park,

Manhattan, the one at Washington Circle, Washington, D.C., the one at Capitol Grounds, Richmond, Virginia, the one at Boston Public Garden, Massachusetts and the one in Place d'Iéna, Paris all have one hoof raised, suggesting that he was wounded in battle and died of his wounds later.

It's sometimes claimed that the convention just applies to the equestrian statues of the battles of Gettysburg, but this is not true either: the equestrian statue of James Longstreet at the Gettysburg National Park shows his horse with one foot raised, yet Longstreet survived the American Civil War, took up politics and died at eighty-three.

There really is no convention for telling the fate of the subject of an equestrian statue. What is most puzzling is that anyone ever believed that there was.

In the Russian Revolution, Bolsheviks stormed the Winter Palace

DURING the Communist revolution of 1917, the Winter Palace in St Petersburg symbolized the excesses of Russian nobility. The March Revolution overthrew the imperial government and the October Revolution placed the Bolsheviks in power. However, during this takeover, the Winter Palace was never stormed, but simply strolled into.

The October Revolution was later presented by the Bolsheviks as a heroic struggle, but in *Lenin and the Russian Revolution*, Steve Phillips reveals that this was 'a gross exaggeration' for the palace was 'not stormed'. In fact, the gates were open and hardly anyone was injured. In *St Petersburg*, Tom Masters records minimal collateral damage: 'Three shells struck the building, bullet holes riddled the square side of the palace and a window was shattered on the third floor.'

Phillips explains that the reason so little force was needed was because 'the Provincial Government held so little power'. By this time, it was 'hardly worth overthrowing'. What is more, in *A History of the Soviet Union from the Beginning to the End*, Peter Kenez reveals that although the besiegers were disorganized and few, this 'did not matter', since the government in the last minutes of its existence 'could count on practically no armed support'.

In his memoir *With the Russian Army, 1914–17*, British officer Alfred W. Knox confirms that the garrison at the Winter Palace 'had dwindled owing to desertions, for there were no provisions and it had been practically starved for two days', adding that 'there was no strong man to take command and to enforce discipline. No one had any stomach for fighting.' Knox reveals that 'the Cossacks left, declaring themselves opposed to bloodshed!' According to Knox, 'at 10 p.m. a large part of the ensigns left, leaving few defenders except the ensigns of the Engineering School and the company of women.'

American-born John Reed recalls in *Ten Days That Shook the World* that at around 2 a.m. the following morning the insurgents flowed 'like a black river, filling all the street, without song or cheer we poured through the Red Arch ... On both sides of the main gateway the doors stood wide open, light streamed out.' He and his comrades were 'swept into the right-hand entrance, opening into a great bare vaulted room'. Reed states that looting began when somebody cried out 'Comrades! Don't take anything! This is the property of the People!'

He adds that 'there was no violence done, although the yunkers [government military officers] were terrified.' The insurgents demanded, 'Will you take up arms against the People any more?' The yunkers promised not to and 'were allowed to go free'.

The entertainment industry seems to have manufactured the storming. Peter Kenez claims that it's so well known to posterity 'from [Sergei] Eisenstein's film *October*'. However, the action 'did not take place as depicted by the great director'. In his essay 'Montage in Theatre and Film', included in Jan van der Eng's work *CCCP*, Dietrich Scheunemann points out that the film's costly central sequence has acquired 'documentary authenticity'.

It is often stated that there is no such thing as a bloodless revolution, but the truth behind this historic event certainly proves otherwise.

Chapter 11

ILLUSORY
INVENTORS

W. H. Hoover invented the vacuum cleaner

THE world's first electrically powered vacuum cleaner
was the size of a milk float. In *The Book of Firsts*, Ian
Harrison reveals that it was so cumbersome it had to be
'mounted on a horse-drawn carriage'. The 1901 invention
of English civil engineer Hubert Cecil Booth had to remain
in the street while 200-metre hoses sucked out the
dust inside the house. However, the innovation in
cleanliness wasn't welcomed by everybody. In
Booth's paper 'The Origin of the Vacuum
Cleaner', published in the 1934–5 edition of
Transactions of the Newcomen Society, he
comments that the police took the view
that his machine 'had no right to
work on a public thoroughfare'.
The unfortunate inventor
was frequently sued for
damages for 'frighten-
ing cab horses in the
street'. Furthermore,
the machine cost £350,

which was prohibitively expensive for the average turn-of-the-century householder, never mind that it wouldn't fit in the cupboard under the stairs.

Booth thought up the vacuuming concept while watching a demonstration of an American cleaning machine. It is often stated that this event occurred in a railway carriage, but Booth cites that it took place at the 'Empire Music Hall'. The apparatus used compressed air to 'blow down into the carpet' and 'drive the dust and air up into the box'. Booth questioned the inventor as to 'why he did not *suck* out the dust'. Unfortunately, the inventor 'became heated', remarking that 'sucking out dust was impossible and that it had been tried over and over again without success; he then walked away.'

Undaunted, Booth considered this conundrum, then 'tried the experiment of sucking with my mouth against the back of a plush seat in a restaurant in Victoria Street.' The upshot: 'I almost choked.' Eureka! . . . kind of . . .

Booth's vacuum cleaner spring-cleaned the Crystal Palace in Hyde Park, London where the men of the Royal Navy Volunteer Reserve were barracked. Twenty-six tons of dust was duly removed, and Booth was advised that 'the health of the men at once improved.' Buoyed by the practical success of his first cleaning contraption, Booth created a new device, the Trolley-Vac, which was put on sale in 1906 priced at thirty-five guineas, but it was still too expensive for the average Edwardian household.

In the USA the following year, James Murray Spangler, an asthmatic janitor from Ohio, patented what *History of Technology* describes as a 'carpet sweeper and cleaner'. Spangler had simply cobbled together a broom handle, a rotating brush and a pillowcase, but what was different about Spangler's sweeper was that he'd attached a small electric motor to it. He happened to show the device to his cousin, Susan Travel Hoover, and as Ian Harrison explains, her husband William H. Hoover, who was a saddler by trade, 'immediately spotted the potential' and bought the rights.

In *The Biographical Dictionary of American Business Leaders* (Volume 2), John N. Hingham explains that Hoover then placed a two-column advertisement in the *Saturday Evening Post*, which read: 'this little machine will take up all the dust and dirt at a cost of less than a penny per room.' His 'little machine' caught on, and in 1926 Hoover further improved the invention by adding a 'beater bar'. *Brewer's Dictionary of Modern Phrase and Fable* explains that 'the name was patented by the company in 1927' and the verb 'to hoover' immediately became part of the English language.

Perhaps it's just as well that William H. Hoover pioneered the device rather than James Murray Spangler. 'I'm just going to Spangler the living room' has a decidedly odd ring to it.

Pythagoras discovered Pythagoras's theorem

FAMILIAR to every school child (I like to think) is the mantra: the square of the hypotenuse of a right-angle triangle is equal to the sum of the squares of the other two sides. In mathematics, Pythagoras's theorem is simply stated as $c^2 = a^2 + b^2$. (Incidentally, don't try learning it from the Tin Man in *The Wizard of Oz*. When he receives his diploma, he proclaims: 'The square of the hypotenuse of an isosceles triangle is equal to the sum of the squares of the other two sides.' No doubt the inclusion of the word 'isosceles' was added to make the theorem sound even more impressive, and indeed the triangle *can* be isosceles (with two sides of equal length), but more importantly, it *must* be right-angled, which the Tin Man neglects to state.)

The famous theorem is routinely credited to sixth-century BCE Greek philosopher and mathematician Pythagoras, but in actual fact, it's difficult to tell Pythagoras's teachings from those of his students, since none of his writings have survived. What's more, his disciples (known as Pythagoreans) were in the habit of supporting their findings by indiscriminately citing their master's authority. In *The*  *Oxford Classical Dictionary,* Fritz Graf agrees that 'in the absence of written records . . . it is impossible to tell how much of the Pythagorean tradition in mathematics, music and astronomy can be traced back to the founder and his early followers.'

First-century BCE Roman architect-engineer Marcus Vitruvius Pollio is the first to link Pythagoras's name with the theorem, but Vitruvius fails to substantiate his claim. In *Measuring Heaven*, Christiane L. Joost-Gaugier suggests he was doing no more than 'recording oral tradition'.

First-century Greek biographer Plutarch quotes mathematician Apollodotus in his work *Moralia*, stating that 'when the famed lines Pythagoras devised, / For which a splendid ox he sacrificed.' However, Plutarch isn't sure whether this tale relates to the above theorem or to the problem 'about the area of the parabolic section of a cone'. He also reports in his essay *The Eating of Flesh* that Pythagoras, a believer in reincarnation and therefore a vegetarian, preached against animal slaughter, so the ox-slaughtering anecdote may be hyperbole on the part of Apollodotus.

The theorem also predates Pythagoras. In *Theory of Algebraic Integers*, Dedkind and Stillwell claim it was 'discovered independently in several different cultures'. The Babylonians 'were fascinated' by such calculations as early as 1800 BCE, apparently recording fifteen of them on a tablet now known as Plympton 322. The *Encyclopaedia Britannica* also cites four Babylonian tablets dating from around 1900–1600 BCE that 'indicate some knowledge of the theorem'. Furthermore, in *The Pyramids,* professor of Egyptology Miroslav Verner reveals that, when constructing the pyramids way back in the twenty-fifth century BCE, the Egyptians 'knew . . . Pythagoras's theorem' although not by that name.

Regardless of its origins, though, Pythagoras's theorem is certainly useful shorthand for expressing the concept. And no oxen were slaughtered in the making of this theorem.

Vyacheslav Molotov invented the Molotov cocktail

S OVIET foreign policy minister Vyacheslav Mikhailovich
Skryabin, to be known henceforth as 'Molotov', was not
the inventor of the renowned Molotov cocktail, but rather the
lesser-known Molotov breadbasket. That's right, breadbasket.

In 1939, at the outbreak of the Second World War, Joseph
Stalin, General Secretary of the Communist Party in the Soviet Union, decided to rearrange his borders with Finland. Not
surprisingly, the Finns were opposed to his actions, and the
Russo-Finnish War resulted. The Finns, taken by surprise,
weren't well equipped to combat Soviet tanks, but they started to deal with the situation by employing petrol bombs first
used during the Spanish Civil War. These homemade bombs
consisted of a bottle filled with petrol containing a length of
rag, which was lit and acted as a fuse. *Brewer's Dictionary of
Modern Phrase and Fable* confirms that Molotov cocktails were
'used by the Finns against the Russians in 1940'. In his 1940

work *My Finnish
Diary*, W. Citrine
reveals that
'when the sol-
diers attack the
Russian tanks,
they call their
rudely-made
hand grenades
"Molotov's cock-
tails".' Thus, as
explained in *A
New Dictionary*

of Eponyms, the explosive cocktail 'was not named to hon-our Molotov' but, as 'a satirical honour for their antagonist – a cocktail for Molotov.'

In *Tank Killing,* author Ian Hogg reveals that in retalia-tion, the Soviet air force bombed Finland with explosives consisting of 'a large container which, after being dropped, split open to shower dozens of incendiary bombs on the target beneath.' The Finns christened these bombs 'Molotov breadbaskets'. (Possibly because Molotov claimed the parcels he was dropping were food parcels and not bombs at all . . . A likely story.)

Fortunately for the Finns, Molotov breadbaskets were singularly ineffective. In *I Was a P-51 Fighter Pilot in WWII,* James Neel White claims that 'snow put out the fires. The bombs missed their targets. Some didn't even hurl the bomblets properly.' Citrine comments that the Finns never even bothered to take cover when the 'Nolotovs' appeared. They even gave the bombs a humorous alternative pronunciation, since '"nolo" is a word which in Finnish is used to describe a rather helpless person who has done something stupid or embarrassing.' White explains that Molotov 'denied having a part in the bomb's creation'.

After Stalin's death in 1953, Vyacheslav Mikhailovich Skryabin fell out of favour and ended up with the dubious honour of being made ambassador to Mongolia.

Robert Bunsen invented the Bunsen Burner

THE Bunsen Burner is a piece of equipment that most people willl remember from school science lessons. It's a small gas burner with a regulating sleeve at the base allowing controlled amounts of air to be added before and after ignition, which has the advantage of producing a hotter flame. The Bunsen Burner was the forerunner of the gas-stove burner and the gas furnace. Nineteenth-century German chemist Robert Bunsen popularized the apparatus in 1855, but the *Macmillan Encyclopedia* reveals that 'he did not, however, invent the Bunsen Burner.'

The first laboratory gas burner was developed by English physicist and chemist Michael Faraday. In his 1827 work *Chemical Manipulations,* Faraday enthuses that 'the chemical gas lamp, which some years ago was a mere curiosity, has now become . . . valuable' since it can be 'adjusted with the utmost nicety in any required position'. *A Dictionary of Physics* explains that Bunsen then employed such a device 'without a regulating sleeve'.

In *The Oxford Companion to the History of Modern Science,* A. J. Rocke reveals that in 1854, Bunsen requested science mechanic Peter Desaga to fashion a burner that would give 'a very hot, sootless, non-luminous flame

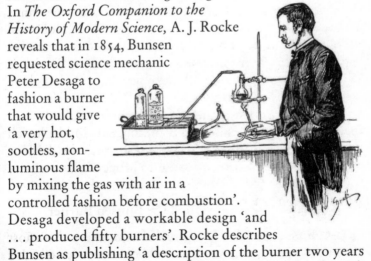

by mixing the gas with air in a controlled fashion before combustion'. Desaga developed a workable design 'and . . . produced fifty burners'. Rocke describes Bunsen as publishing 'a description of the burner two years later', and the new improved burner was quickly adopted.

Desaga never did patent his invention, 'in effect donating this important invention to the world of science'.

What a valuable addition to modern science practice those burners turned out to be – unlike the small mats they stood upon, which I used to chew in bored moments in my chemistry lessons and which, I later discovered, were fashioned from the finest asbestos.

The Marquess of Queensberry invented the Queensberry Rules

BEFORE the British Boxing Board of Control established boxing rules in 1929, the sport was effectively governed by what was known as the Queensberry Rules, which were introduced in 1867. Among other things, these rules stipulated a three-minute round and a ten-second count after a knockdown. However, most importantly, the rules also forbad bare-knuckle boxing; specially-made boxing gloves had to be worn. Previously, the London Prize Ring Rules of 1839 were the only boxing rules in operation.

The Queensberry Rules may bear his name, but John Sholto Douglas, 9th Marquess of Queensberry, did not draw them up. He merely endorsed them. In 1866, Queensberry toured the United States with British amateur athlete John Graham Chambers to promote the art of boxing. During this tour, Chambers formulated the rules under Queensberry's supervision and they were published the following year.

Queensberry was, himself, an amateur boxer of note, although an entry in the *Oxford Dictionary of National Biography* reveals that he was far from the epitome of good conduct. In 1872, for example, he was 'fined twenty shillings

by Bow Street magistrates for assaulting a man who had attempted to prevent him assaulting a hotel porter.' *A New Dictionary of Eponyms* adds that 'because Chambers performed yeoman service in devising the rules, some believe that his is the name that should have been honoured instead of Queensberry's.'

In practice, the Marquess of Queensberry is more famous for threatening to horsewhip Lord Rosebery, and for winning a libel case against the lover of his son Alfred, namely writer and wit Oscar Wilde.

Chapter 12

LESS-THAN-LIKELY LAST WORDS

**Queen Elizabeth I's last words were
'All my possessions for a moment of time'**

IF you had to think up poignant yet philosophical final words for a dying monarch, these would surely be they, and it would appear that this is precisely what happened in Queen Elizabeth's case. The *Oxford Dictionary of Quotations* states that these famous words are 'almost certainly apocryphal', since witnesses to the Queen's death make no mention of them.

The seventy-year-old monarch had a drawn-out demise, halfway through which she lost the powers of speech due to what her maid of honour, Elizabeth Southwell, described as 'a sower throt' in her 1607 essay *A True Relation of What Succeeded at the Sickness and Death of Queen Elizabeth*. Without any trusty throat sweets to suck on in the early seventeenth century, the Queen was thus prevented from uttering any 'good' last words. In fact, according to law student John Manningham in his 1603 diary, he had it on good authority that just before her death, the Queen 'hath been in a manner speechless for two days'. *The Mysteries of Elizabeth I* reveals that 'when Elizabeth was no longer able to speak, she responded to religious exultations with gestures.' In his 1603 sermon *God's Universal Right Proclaimed*, John Hayward confirms this by explaining that the Queen died 'testifying her joy with her hand, which she could not so well do with her voice'.

Southwell suggests that Queen Elizabeth's actual last words were complaints about the gaggle of clergy repeatedly requiring her, during her protracted demise, to make her peace with God. This appears to have caused her great annoyance since, with a reputation as a lifelong virgin, she did not feel she was in the least bit of spiritual danger with the Almighty. Southwell describes Elizabeth, when she could speak, suggesting that these 'hedge priests . . . be packing' since she 'tok yt for an yndignite that they should speak to her'. Rather than requiring a 'moment of time', Elizabeth probably would have benefited from a less protracted death, thereby saving her from the irritating ministrations of her overzealous clergy.

William Pitt the Younger's last words were 'Oh my country! How I leave my country'

IN 1806, British Prime Minister William Pitt the Younger died in office worrying about Napoleon overrunning Europe, as the French emperor's impressive victory over the Austrians and Prussians at Austerlitz had, according to Michael Macdonagh in *Parliament,* 'cast a shadow over the nations rejoicing the victory of Trafalgar'.

The official story was that Pitt the Younger uttered the above words with his final gasp, and it is possible that he did say them at some point during his last hours. However, Macdonagh and Daisy Sampson (editor of *The Politics Companion*) both relate that future PM Benjamin Disraeli heard of a different version of events, which revealed Pitt's actual last words to be altogether more prosaic. Macdonagh quotes Disraeli describing how an old waiter at the House of Commons had confided to him that he had once been called out of bed 'by a messenger in a post chaise, shouting to me outside the window.' Apparently, the messenger instructed the waiter: 'Bring one of your pork pies down to Mr Pitt at Putney.' As they were conveying the said pork pie, the messenger revealed to the waiter that Pitt, gravely ill, had rather optimistically said, 'I think I could eat one of Bellamy's [long-standing caterer to the House of Parliament] pork pies.' The waiter promptly delivered the pie but, sadly, Pitt the Younger had already passed on and never got to sample it.

King George V's last words were 'How's the Empire?' or 'Bugger Bognor'

IN a similar vein to Pitt the Younger, in 1936 the welfare of the Empire was said to be the final concern of the dying King, and *The Times* reported his last words as 'How's the Empire?' (Wits have since suggested that he was simply enquiring 'What's on at the Empire?') In *King George V,* biographer Kenneth Rose explains that these words *were*

said, but only on the morning of his demise as he was reading the paper: they were not his final utterance.

It is also regularly claimed that the King's dying words were 'Bugger Bognor'. Rose relates that seven years earlier, after a serious illness, the King went to the coastal resort of Bognor in Sussex for three months' convalescence. In an effort to reassure him, despite being on his deathbed, his doctors remarked, 'Cheer up, your

Majesty, you will soon be at Bognor again.' The King is said to have replied, 'Bugger Bognor' and promptly expired. In *The Lives of the Kings and Queens of England*, however, Antonia Fraser dismisses this tale as a 'myth'. She reveals that a Privy Council was foisted onto the dying King, and when he felt capable of speaking, he stated 'Gentlemen . . . I am sorry for keeping you waiting like that. I am unable to concentrate.' Both Fraser and Rose agree that these words were, in reality, the last the King ever spoke.

'Bugger Bognor' was very possibly uttered, but the phrase most likely dates back to the convalescent stay when, according to Rose, a deputation of leading citizens made a request to King George. On the strength of his stay, they requested that 'their salubrious town should henceforth be known as Bognor Regis [Royal Bognor]'. Rose suggests that the offending comment could have been privately uttered at this point by the King. Either way, the deputation was politely informed that the King 'would be graciously pleased to grant their request'. Bognor has ever since been known as Bognor Regis, and it's as good a place as any to go to die.

Nelson's final words were 'Kiss me, Hardy'

DURING the Battle of Trafalgar in 1805, British naval commander Viscount Horatio Nelson was right in the thick of it. As related in *Nelson's Surgeon*, at about 1.15 p.m. the ship's surgeon Dr William Beatty comments that Nelson was pacing the quarterdeck of his ship, the *Victory*, with his flag captain Thomas Masterman Hardy, when he

was hit by a musket-ball fired from the mizzen-mast of the French *Redoubtable*: 'The ball struck the epaulette on his left shoulder, and penetrated his chest.'

Nelson was rushed below deck, but it was soon clear that he was dying. Literary scholar and biographer Robert Southey records in his 1896 work *The Life of Nelson* that Nelson then said, 'Kiss me, Hardy,' and 'Hardy knelt down and kissed his cheek.' This show of affection, seen as entirely proper at the time, disconcerted late Victorians who thought it best to conjecture that what Nelson had actually said was 'Kismet, Hardy.' (*Kismet* comes from the Turkish/Arabic word *qisma*, meaning 'portion' or 'lot'.) It's a neat-sounding theory, but the *OED* reveals that *kismet* wasn't recorded in Britain until around fifty years later (when E. B. Eastwick wrote in *Dry Leaves*, 'One day a man related to me a story of kismet or destiny').

Modern historians, including those at the Nelson Society, agree that the dying British admiral did indeed ask Hardy to kiss him before he died, but these were not his final words. Indeed, after this touching farewell, Hardy left the scene and was not even present during Nelson's final moments.

Beatty records that Nelson became thirsty, and called for 'drink, drink'. He also asked for 'fan, fan' and 'rub, rub'. He was 'addressing himself in the last case to Dr Scott, who had been rubbing his lordship's breast, with his hand, from which he had found some relief.' Beatty describes how Nelson continued to say these words again and again 'till a very few minutes before he expired', adding that Nelson then 'pronounced distinctly these final words: "Thank God, I have done my duty."' According to Beatty, he repeated these words several times until he became unable to speak.

Whichever you like to consider as Nelson's actual last words, 'Thank God, I have done my duty' or 'Drink, drink. Fan, fan. Rub, rub,' none seem to be as popular as the words most commonly attributed to him, namely 'Kiss me, Hardy.'

Chapter 13

DUBIOUS
DISCOVERERS

**Benjamin Franklin flew a kite into a thunderstorm
to prove lightning is electrical**

IN the mid eighteenth century,
American statesman, scientist and inventor Benjamin
Franklin became interested
in the latest fad: electricity.
In 1751, Franklin's theo-
ries about drawing
meteorological electricity
from storms using metal
rods were published, but
before he could test them
out, Frenchman Georges-
Louis Leclerc de Buffon stole
his thunder, so to speak, by
beating him to it in France.

Buffon wasn't daft enough to test the rig himself. In *The
Oxford Companion to the History of Modern Science*, J. L.
Heilbron reveals that during a storm, he employed the
services of a 'dispensable old soldier' who obligingly

'approached his knuckle to the rod [and] drew a spark'. Heilbron explains that the veteran survived thanks to the fact that the rod picked up only minor electrical fluctuations rather than a full-blown lightning strike, which would have fried him . . . as we shall see later.

Kites, rather than metal rods, then became the favoured conductors. Heilbron suggests that French scientist Jacques de Romas was 'the first to propose to bring atmospheric charge to earth via a kite'. In a letter to Peter Collinson, dated October 1752, Franklin claimed that the French experiment had 'succeeded in Philadelphia' using a kite, a metal key, silk ribbon and a Leyden jar, which Franklin refers to as a 'phial'. Franklin explained that the wet kite string would 'conduct the electric fire freely', then to the end of the string 'next the hand, is to be tied a silk ribbon'; where the silk and string join

'a key may be fastened'. The kite was to be raised 'when a thunder-gust appears to be coming on', and the experimenter 'must stand within a door or window, or under some cover, so that the silk ribbon may not be wet; and care must be taken that the twine does not touch the frame of the door or window.' (Franklin incorporated the decidedly insubstantial safety device of the dry, silk ribbon to prevent the experimenter from frying.) Electricity will then 'stream out plentifully from the key at the approach of your knuckle'. The experimenter can then charge 'the phial' with the resulting electricity conduced through the key. (The phial or Leyden jar was an electrical condenser.) You will note that Franklin sensibly suggests collecting the electrical charge into the 'Leyden jar' rather than the experimenter. In effect, Franklin was making use of the kite string to elevate the metal key into the storm. It was the 'key' that was to conduct the charge, not the person on the end of the wet string.

In *History and Present State of Electricity,* British scientist Joseph Priestley claimed in 1767 that Franklin performed this experiment in June 1755, although he left no account of it. Priestley described how, 'a month after the electricians in France had verified the same theory', Franklin stood in a shed, in a field, and 'presented his knuckle to the key'. Seemingly unaware of the possible effect of such a practice, Priestley then invites the reader to judge the 'exquisite pleasure he [Franklin] must have felt at that moment' when the scientist 'perceived a very evident electric spark'. (Priestley had obviously never been on the end of a live lamp cable, which he believed, mistakenly, to be unplugged.)

R. Conrad Stein, a biographer of Benjamin Franklin, states that 'no one is absolutely sure whether or not Franklin actually performed it.' One thing we do know is that Franklin did not simply fly an unmodified kite directly into a thunderstorm to see what happened.

The next year, on the strength of Franklin's lightning rod findings, German physicist Georg Wilhelm Richmann constructed with fatal consequences a DIY lightning rod. In *Ball Lightning*, Mark Stenhoff reveals that on sighting an approaching storm, Richmann raced home with a colleague to try some experiments. The colleague explained that no sooner had the professor approached the lightning rod than 'a palish blue ball of fire, as big as a fist, came out of the rod.' Unfortunately, 'it went right to the forehead of the professor, who in that instant fell back without uttering a sound.' His colleague reported that the professor's shoes 'burst open' where the deadly charge had made its way to earth through his feet. So much for hotfooting it home to experiment with lightning.

Alexander Fleming discovered penicillin on mouldy bread in his laboratory

THE development of penicillin in the first half of the twentieth century is arguably the greatest medical leap forward of modern times. In 1928, Scottish bacteriologist Alexander Fleming discovered this 'magic bullet' by accident. In his 1945 Nobel Lecture, published in *Nobel Lectures in Physiology or Medicine 1942–62*, he admits that 'penicillin started as a chance observation'. At the time, Fleming was working on a flu cure when he discovered the fortunate find on a discarded Petri dish, rather than his leftover lunch. In his 1929 work 'On the Antibacterial

Action of Cultures of a Penicillium', published in the *British Journal of Experimental Pathology,* Fleming explains that 'in the examinations, these plates were necessarily exposed to the air and they became contaminated with various micro-organisms.' (In truth, Fleming's laboratory was generally in chaos and experimental Petri dishes were left lying around for weeks on end.)

The contaminating mould is sometimes said to have floated in through an open window. In fact, the spores wafted up from the laboratory below where they were conducting allergy tests. Bread became linked to the story because the mould in question was bread mould. Since the mould growth (spores of *Penicillium notatum*) appeared to kill the bacteria on the Petri dish, Fleming concluded it

must have 'bactericidal' properties. He continues: 'My only merit is that I did not neglect the observation and that I pursued the subject as a bacteriologist.'

However, it seems he didn't pursue it very far since an entry in *Who's Who in the Twentieth Century* reveals that Fleming 'failed to produce a pure extract or demonstrate its true therapeutic value'. *Encyclopaedia Britannica* puts this down to Fleming's lack of 'the necessary chemical means to isolate and identify the active compound involved.' While J. K. Aronson in *The Oxford Companion to Medicine* adds that Fleming 'made no efforts to apply it clinically'. Even Fleming confesses that 'my publication in 1929 was the starting-point of the work of others who developed penicillin especially in the chemical field.'

In fact, according to *Who's Who in the Twentieth Century*, it was not until 1940 that Ernst Chain and Howard Florey proved 'its enormous value as an antibiotic . . . [and] their work paved the way for numerous other antibiotics and a revolution in the treatment of bacterial and fungal diseases.'

Possibly, we regard penicillin solely as Fleming's discovery thanks to Sir Almroth Wright's letter of 28 August 1942, which states that the 'laurel wreath' for discovering penicillin 'should be decreed to Professor Alexander Fleming of this research laboratory'. Clearly, Almroth was eager to garner credit for his inoculation department at St Mary's Hospital in Paddington, London. Sir Almroth goes on to state that Fleming 'is the discoverer of penicillin and was the author also of the original suggestion that this substance might prove to have important applications in medicine'. However, the scientific community was clearly more aware of the true state of affairs, since Fleming, Florey and Chain all shared the 1945 Nobel Prize in physiology or medicine.

Edmond Halley discovered Halley's Comet

G REAT balls of fire whooshing through the sky are often difficult to miss. The world's most famous comet was sighted and documented over 2,000 years ago by Chinese astronomers who spotted it in 240 BCE. Its closest approach to Earth was in 837. The *Illustrated Dictionary of Science* reveals that the comet is 'featured on the Bayeux tapestry' of 1066. King Harold can be seen ducking while his courtiers point in wonderment at the fireball.

It is sometimes suggested that the Star of Bethlehem was an appearance of the comet, but astronomer Patrick Moore sets the record straight in *The Data Book of Astronomy* by pointing out 'it returned years too early' in 12 BCE. In a biography of Edmond Halley, Alan Cook suggests that its appearance in 1301 inspired Italian painter Giotto di Bondone to depict a large fireball as the Star of Bethlehem above the stable in his religious fresco *Adoration of the Magi* (1304–06).

Early eighteenth-century English astronomer Edmond Halley was simply the first to calculate the orbit, identify it as the same comet and correctly predict its reappearance. In his 1705 work *A Synopsis of the Astronomy of Comets,* he showed that the comets which had appeared in 1531, 1607 and 1682 (when he first saw it) were the same comet, appearing at roughly seventy-six-year intervals: 'Hence I dare venture to foretell, that it will return again in the year 1758.'

Sadly, Halley died in 1742 before he could be proved correct, but the successful reappearance of the comet resulted in it being named after him sixteen years after his death. Halley's Comet is next expected to return to the inner solar system in 2061, by which time, no doubt, health and safety regulations will advise us not to look at it in case it gives someone a bit of a headache.

Charles Darwin delayed publication of his theory of evolution for fear of ostracism

FAMED for his theory of evolution by natural selection, nineteenth-century naturalist Charles Darwin first formulated his ideas around 1840, but he didn't publish his findings in *On the Origin of Species by Means of Natural Selection* until 1859, almost twenty years later. It is generally stated that fear of public and private ridicule and reprisals paralysed Darwin into holding back from publication, and it is often said that he kept his findings on evolution a close secret.

Yet, Darwin makes no mention of this fear or secrecy in his blithe *Autobiography*, which he penned in 1876 (never

intended for publication). Cambridge science historian Dr John van Wyhe claims that 'Darwin's delay is a recent historiographical theme for which there is no clear evidence.' In his 2007 research paper, 'Mind the Gap: Did Darwin Avoid Publishing his Paper for Many Years?' Van Wyhe states that this popular theory is 'overwhelmingly contradicted by the historical evidence', adding that Darwin's belief 'was not a secret before publication'. Indeed, in an 1844 letter, Darwin announced to botanist Joseph Dalton Hooker: 'I think I have found out (here's presumption!) the simple way by which species become exquisitely adapted to various ends.'

Darwin was aware that many would find fault with his theories. He commented to Hooker that his belief in evolution was 'like confessing a murder'. However, rather than fearing ridicule, when publishing his 1841 findings on the discovery of erratic boulders in South America, Darwin wrote in an 1848 letter to geologist John Phillips: 'I believe I shall get well abused for my paper & not make single convert to my own view, but I am resolved not to show a white feather & bring it out.'

Britannica states that 'the idea of evolution was not new.' Darwin's theory simply 'explained how evolution occurred'. In his autobiography, Darwin explains that in 1837 'I opened my first note-book for facts in relation to the Origin of Species, about which I had long reflected, and never ceased working for the next twenty years.' Darwin wrote a brief sketch of his theory in 1842, followed by a longer one in 1844, but it was not until 1856 that he began his 'multivolume work on evolution', which was more than sixteen years after he formulated the theory.

In *Origins of Genius*, Dean Keith Simonton reveals that 'friends like the geologist Charles Lyell advised Darwin not to procrastinate too long, for fear that he might be pre-empted by some other scientist.' This is precisely what happened. In June 1858, Darwin had completed a quarter of a million words when, as he explains in his autobiography, English specimen collector Alfred Russel Wallace 'sent me an essay "On the Tendency of Varieties to depart indefinitely from the Original Type".' According to Darwin: 'This essay contained exactly the same theory as mine.'

Forgotten Ideas, Neglected Pioneers by Daniel L. Schacter quotes Darwin opining to Lyell that 'your words have come true with a vengeance – that I should be fore-stalled . . . so that all my originality, whatever it may amount to, will be smashed.' Consequently, Darwin published jointly with Wallace just two weeks after he received the letter. The joint publication, Darwin noted, 'excited very little attention'.

Darwin then published *On the Origin of Species,* writing to Lyell that he was 'a very slow thinker, for you would be surprised at the number of years it took me to see clearly what some of the problems were, which had to be solved.' *Origin* does not speculate on man's origins; *Britannica* reveals that it was 'the newspapers [that] drew the one conclusion that Darwin had specifically avoided: that humans had evolved from apes.' In Darwin's view, as 'many naturalists fully accepted the doctrine of the evolution of species, it seemed to me advisable to work up such notes as I possessed, and to publish a special treatise on the origin of man.' Three years before *Descent of Man* was published in 1871, the King of Prussia conferred on Darwin 'the *order Pour le Mérite*'.

During Darwin's lifetime 'the scientific community largely accepted his theory of descent,' according to *Britannica*, 'though it was slower to adopt his idea of natural selection.'

Chapter 14

MISATTRIBUTED QUOTES

It was Voltaire who said 'I disapprove of what you say, but I will defend to the death your right to say it'

EIGHTEENTH-CENTURY French writer and philosopher Voltaire supposedly uttered these famed words to fellow philosopher Claude-Adrien Helvétius, after Helvétius's heretical 1758 book *De l'esprit* (*On the Mind*) was publicly burnt by the hangman. However, the phrase does not appear in Voltaire's extensive writings. In his 1881 *Life of Voltaire*, biographer James Parton suggests that what Voltaire actually said on the occasion of the book burning was 'What a fuss about an omelette!' The great thinker hadn't taken the opportunity to prepare lunch over the blazing

volume: he was simply implying that the book-burning was an overreaction.

Though Voltaire was a champion of free speech, *Encyclo-paedia Britannica* reveals that on this occasion he referred to Helvétius's book as 'commonplace, obscure, and in error'.

Regarding the famous misattributed quotation, it is true that Voltaire did pen statements of a similar sentiment. In his 1763 *Essay on Tolerance*, he wrote 'Think for yourselves and let others enjoy the privilege to do so too.' *A Book of French Quotations* quotes Voltaire stating in a 1770 letter to Monsieur le Riche: 'I detest what you write, but I would give my life to make it possible for you to continue to write.' Neither is as succinct as the more familiar quote, but the opinion being expressed is the same.

The *Oxford Dictionary of Quotations* reveals that the phrase was first coined by English writer Evelyn Beatrice Hall (writing under the pseudonym of S. G. Tallentyre) in her 1906 work *Friends of Voltaire*. Marjorie Garber explains in *Quotation Marks* that Hall never intended to imply that Voltaire said the famed quote. By writing the quote 'in double quotation marks' Hall was attempting to quantify how Voltaire was thinking, and her choice of punctuation merely signified her interpretation of Voltaire's beliefs. Garber confirms that when Hall was questioned about the quote many years after her book was published, she explained that 'she had not intended to imply that Voltaire used those words verbatim, and would be very surprised if they were to be found in any of his works.' Hall clearly approved of what Voltaire had to say; so much so that she accidentally assisted him in his attempt to say it.

US Patent Office Commissioner Charles H. Duell said 'Everything that can be invented has been invented'

MUCH-DERIDED US patent officer Charles H. Duell is regularly referred to as an idiot bureaucrat for making such a preposterous statement. In 1899, his views are said to have either prompted him to write to President McKinley urging him to close the Patent Office or to have offered his resignation, since he believed that no more inventions could be expected. Samuel Sass reveals in a 1989 *Skeptical Inquirer* article that a Dr Eber Jeffery made a full investigation of the matter. In a 1940 edition of the *Journal of the Patent Office Society,* Jeffery states that he 'found no evidence that any official or employee of the US Patent Office had ever resigned because he thought there was nothing left to invent': quite the opposite, in fact. It would even appear that Duell's 1899 report documented an *increase* of about 3,000 patents over the previous year.

In *From Wall Street to China*, authors Worrall and O'Shea also confirm that 'the story is not true'. Jeffrey states that the mythical speech stems from fellow patent officer, Henry L. Ellsworth. In 1843, Ellsworth declared to the US Congress that 'the advancement of the arts, from year to year, taxes our credulity and seems to presage the arrival of that period when human improvement must end.' Ellsworth's words, however, appear to have been pure rhetoric since, like all good bureaucrats, he went on to suggest that the Patent Office receive further investment to fund future expansion. Sass claims that when Ellsworth resigned two years later, he gave as his reason 'the pressure of private affairs' and stated 'I wish to express a willingness that others may share public favours and have an opportunity to make greater improvements.'

Thus, it appears that the quote about there being nothing left to invent was itself pure invention.

Edmund Burke said 'It is necessary only for the good man to do nothing for evil to triumph'

EIGHTEENTH-CENTURY Anglo-Irish statesman Edmund Burke is regularly quoted as having penned these wise words. However, *The Concise Oxford Dictionary of Quotations* points out that the quote is 'not found in his writings'.

In *They Never Said It*, Paul F. Boller says that the fourteenth edition of *Bartlett's Familiar Quotations* claimed the famous words were allegedly written in a letter to William Smith on 9 January 1795. However, Boller reveals that upon closer investigation, the letter was found to be dated 29 January and it made no reference to the triumph of evil. He adds that when *New York Times* columnist William Safire approached *Bartlett's* editor about the issue, he was advised that the statement could not be located 'so far'.

Burke did voice a similar statement, however, when he delivered a parliamentary speech in 1770 entitled *Thoughts on the Cause of the Present Discontents.* In it he claimed, 'When bad men combine, the good must associate; else they will fall, one by one, an unpitied sacrifice in a contemptible struggle,' which appears to mirror the general sentiment of the famous misattributed quote . . . I think.

During the Battle of Waterloo, the Duke of Wellington exclaimed 'Up, guards, and at 'em'

SIR ARTHUR WELLESLEY, the Duke of Wellington, was reported to have shouted this command to his men, the British Foot Guards, just before the Battle of Waterloo, which was fought in Belgium in 1815 against Napoleonic forces.

The *Concise Oxford Dictionary of Quotations* explains that the quotation was originally related in a letter written by an officer in the Guards, but that it was 'later denied by Wellington'. In *They Never Said It*, Paul F. Boller agrees that 'the Duke denied he ever uttered that cry'. It is explained that 'at one point, when the guards were lying down, as they customarily did under fire . . . he ordered them to rise.' According to *The Oxford Companion to Military History*, what the Iron Duke actually shouted was 'Up Guards! Make ready! Fire!'

Whatever Wellington said to his men, it did the trick. With the help of the Prussians, the formidable Emperor Napoleon was narrowly defeated and finally met his Waterloo.

Benjamin Disraeli said 'There are three sorts of lies: lies, damned lies and statistics'

Tʜɪs much-quoted saying means that statistics, if mis-used, can be deeply misleading. It is generally attributed to British Prime Minister Benjamin Disraeli.

In his 1924 *Autobiography*, Mark Twain commented 'the remark attributed to Disraeli would often apply with justice and force: "There are three kinds of lies: lies, damned lies, and statistics."'

Yet, *The Columbia World of Quotations* points out intriguingly that 'the words have never been found among Disraeli's works.' The *Oxford Dictionary of Scientific Quotations* also reveals that 'there is no further evidence beyond this attribution that Disraeli made this statement.'

It's not clear who did coin the phrase. In *Respectfully Quoted*, Suzy Platt suggests that journalist and politician Henry Labouchère might have been the true originator. Other candidates include US Congressman Abram S. Hewitt and naval serviceman and author

Holloway H. Frost. Although Disraeli originated many a wise saying, this, it appears, was not one of them.

Winston Churchill said 'Naval tradition? Nothing but rum, sodomy and the lash'

WHEN an admiral protested that the provision of better conditions for ordinary seaman was 'against the traditions' of the Royal Navy, British Prime Minister Winston Churchill is alleged to have given this famous reply. Yet, according to the Churchill Centre's publication *Finest Hour* (Spring 2006), when Churchill's private secretary Sir Anthony Montague-Browne 'confronted Churchill with this quotation' while they were at dinner, Montague-Browne reported that Churchill replied, 'I never said it. I wish I had.'

The original exchange is allegedly recorded in *The Harold Nicolson Diaries: 1919–64*, in which the 17 July 1950 entry is said to quote the phrase, but the copy I consulted jumped from 28 July to 23 September with no mention of rum, sodomy or even lash. *In Search of Churchill* author, Martin Gilbert, recounts how he himself once gave a 'graphic rendering of this reply (though it does not appear in any of my volumes) during an evening reception in Chicago, only to be unexpectedly and forcibly rebuked by my host, a retired ambassador, who insisted that the story was apocryphal.' Gilbert confesses that he 'felt ashamed to have been caught telling it, being so scornful myself of unauthenticated stories.'

The *Oxford Dictionary of Quotations* casts light on a possible origin of the phrase by recording a naval saying dating from the nineteenth century, which ran: 'Ashore it's wine, women and song, aboard it's rum, bum and concertina.' Feel free to draw your own conclusions as to what that might have meant . . .

King Louis XV of France said 'Après moi le déluge' ('After me the flood')

THE correct form of the quote, which runs *'Après nous le déluge'* ('After us the flood'), is generally understood to mean: I don't care or I dread to think what will happen after we are/I am gone. In her 1824 *Mémoires*, Madame du Hausset reveals that it was said by the King's favourite mistress Madame de Pompadour. *The Dictionary of Women's Biography* agrees that Madame de Pompadour 'is credited with the famous remark'. *The Oxford Essential Dictionary of Foreign Terms in English* explains that she spoke these words 'after the French defeat by the Prussians at Rossbach in 1757', which heralded the end of the *ancien régime*.

Interestingly, though, it seems that Madame de Pompadour did not originate the phrase. John Farquhar Shaw's work *A New Dictionary of Quotations* reveals that the origin of the saying was an old French proverb.

Chapter 15

PHONEY PHRASE ORIGINS

Roman soldiers were paid in salt hence the saying 'worth his salt'

SALT was greatly valued in Roman times, and as Jonathan P. Roth reveals in *The Logistics of the Roman Army at War*, it formed 'a very important part of the soldiers' diet.' This was not simply because their rations needed seasoning: Romans believed salt to be vital to good health. For example, in *Roman History*, Greek historian Appian of Alexandria explains how Roman soldiers in Lucullus's army in second-century BCE Spain ate 'the flesh of deer and rabbits boiled without salt, which caused dysentery, from which many died.'

Salt was therefore considered a vital resource, but it was never used as a form of payment. It's true that the word 'salary' derives from the Latin for salt, but this is not because Roman soldiers were paid in salt; they were paid in money. This was their *stipendium*, from which we get the word 'stipend' which isn't much used nowadays but, as the *Oxford English Dictionary* (*OED*) explains, used to mean the pay of a soldier and also of clergymen, schoolmasters, judges and the like. In *Thereby Hangs a Tale*, lexicographer

Charles E. Funk explains that each Roman soldier, when sent abroad, was given an allowance 'over and above his regular pay' to be used specifically 'for the purchase of salt'. Funk claims that the amount varied because 'salt might be hard to get and expensive in one country, but cheap and plentiful in another.' The *OED* confirms that the Latin word *salarium* originally equated to 'money allowed to Roman soldiers for the purchase of salt'. Funk states that *salarium* later became a term for 'the sum of money which a military officer or a governor of a province . . . received at intervals, in addition to various supplies in kind.' The word eventually became synonymous with a payment for work.

The *Dictionary of Idioms* reveals that the saying 'worth his salt', despite sounding ancient, dates back merely to 'the first half of the nineteenth century'. The *OED* cites the first known reference to 1830, when Frederick Marryat wrote 'The captain . . . is not worth his salt' in his work *King's Own*. In the *Wordsworth Dictionary of Idioms*, Catherine M. Schwarz suggests that the 'salt' of the saying may refer to that eaten 'by a servant'. Far from dating back to ancient Rome, then, the phrase is merely of Victorian origin. Hardly worth its salt!

'Dead ringer', 'Saved by the bell' and 'Working the graveyard shift' originate from Victorian graveyard rescues

THE morbid fear of being buried alive predates the Victorians and was rife in the late eighteenth century. In *Glory and Terror*, Antoine De Baecque reveals that in France, recommendations to avoid such a fate were to be found in the 1787 pamphlet *Reflections on the Danger of Being Buried Alive*. The deceased was to be dressed warmly and furnished with 'a piece of bread and a flask of good wine'. The reader was advised to ensure that 'the cork extends above the neck of the bottle far enough so that it can be easily uncorked'. (Those finding themselves prematurely interred would surely baulk at the added inconvenience of not being able to uncork the wine.) 'To the right fist of the body will be attached a bell cord that passes through its hand, and that leaves the coffin through a little hole.' The bell was hooked up to a 'cord . . . attached to a post embedded in the ground to the right of the coffin'. This must surely have been one of the very first coffin alarms.

Professor Jan Bondeson's fascinating work *Buried Alive* tells how eighteenth-century German parson P. G. Pessler suggested the cord could be connected to the church bell. A touch too ambitious, perhaps, as quite a hefty tug would have been needed to set off the alarm. To remedy this, fellow German inventor Johann Georg Hypelli came up with an alarm placed above the head of the deceased. If the occupant revived and tried to sit up, the resultant impact onto the alarm would set it off automatically. What an improvement! Patented alarmed coffins such as the Bateson Life Revival Device went into production in 1852.

It's easy to see how these measures gave rise to the above legends: if you rang the bell, you were a 'dead ringer'; if somebody heard your alarm, you were 'saved by the bell'. Relatives, allegedly posted to sit at the graveside, were said to be doing the 'graveyard shift'. Nevertheless, claims that these phrases originated from the use of coffin alarms are false.

The *OED* defines 'dead ringer' as American in origin, dating back to around 1891. A clue that it's a misinterpretation lies in the meaning of the phrase. It has nothing to do with cheating death, but simply means 'to very closely resemble'. The dead part has a similar meaning to 'complete' or 'absolute' as in 'dead heat', 'dead loss' or 'dead right'.

'Saved by the bell' does indeed mean being saved from an unpleasant occurrence by a timely intervention, but this saying wasn't in use during Victorian times. It dates to the 1930s and is a boxing term. The 1932 publication *Ring* describes 'the bell' saving 'the Jersey boy at the count of seven'. The *Oxford Dictionary of Phrase and Fable* confirms that the phrase stems from the boxing match convention that 'a floored contestant can be saved from being counted out by the ringing of the bell to mark the end of a round.'

It was, of course, the graveyard workers who monitored the coffin alarms, not the grieving relatives. Indeed, if relatives had even the smallest inkling that the deceased wasn't completely dead, let's hope they held off the burial until they felt more definite about the matter. The *OED* dates the term 'graveyard shift' to the 1900s when it simply meant the night shift. *Phrase and Fable* suggests 'the term is originally nautical, and has been explained as referring to the number of disasters that occur during this time.'

You're bound to be wondering: were people really buried alive? Bondeson reveals that 'there are . . . a few accounts, confirmed by reliable medical professionals, of people actually buried alive who recovered in their coffins and called assistance by knocking on the lid.' He adds scarily that this phenomenon, for obvious reasons, could well be under-reported. Cremations all round, everyone?

'Sleep tight' and 'tying the knot' originate from the ropes on medieval bedsteads

THIS is a favourite with tour guides. It's sometimes said of hammocks aboard ships, which are supposed to have afforded a better night's sleep if tightly strung. It's true that medieval bedsteads were under-strung with rope and a mattress was placed on top. The knotted bed base is said to be responsible for the phrase 'tying the knot', since it is jocularly suggested that the ropes needed to be good and tight to support the happy couple on their wedding night.

However, though the phrase 'tying the knot' is connected to marriage, it has nothing to do with bedsteads. It is an old expression that dates back to the thirteenth century.

The *OED* points out that it meant 'the tie or bond of wed-lock'. In Shakespeare's play *Romeo and Juliet*, Juliet's father, trying to hasten Juliet's arranged marriage, issues the order: 'Send for the Countie . . . I'll have this knot knit up tomorrow morning.'

In *The Real McCoy: A Dictionary of Peculiar English*, Peter Chadington reveals that the first written reference to 'sleep tight' is from Susan Eppes's 1866 diary *Through Some Eventful Years*. She writes: 'Goodbye little Diary. "Sleep tight and wake bright," for I will need you when I return.' The *OED* explains that the eighteenth- and nineteenth-century meaning of 'tight' or 'tightly' meant 'roundly' or 'soundly', in other words, properly or effectively. Chadington agrees that tight 'was applied to sleep from the end of the eighteenth century, and meant "soundly".' The phrase 'sleep tight' simply meant 'sleep well'.

Thus, neither of these sayings derive from any form of bedstead maintenance.

'Running the gauntlet' originates from a military punishment involving medieval fighting gloves

RUNNING the gauntlet was indeed a military punishment, but gloves didn't figure in the procedure. The culprit had to run between two rows of men whose job it was to brandish sticks or knotted cords at him. In his 1676 work *The History of King Philip's War*, seventeenth-century American Puritan minister Increase Mather relates a case involving a number of men where 'they stripped them naked, and caused them to run the Gauntlet.' Nowadays, thank goodness, it's merely used figuratively, and means having to undergo an arduous trial (usually physical).

As the *OED* confirms, a gauntlet is 'a glove worn as part of medieval armour, usually made of leather, covered with plates of steel.' The word derives from the French *gantelet* and *gant,* meaning glove, and to throw down the gauntlet was a challenge to a duel.

However, the gauntlet in the 'running the gauntlet' phrase is not a glove but a corruption of *gantlope*. One careful writer, the 1st Earl of Shaftesbury, wrote in his 1646 diary, 'Three were condemned to die, two to run the gantelope.' Regarding the definition of *gantelope*, it's a corruption of the Swedish *gatlopp*, which originated from its forerunner *gata* and *lopp*. This approximates, as you might expect, to 'path' and 'run'. Offenders were simply 'running the pathway'; nothing to do with being bashed by gloves at all.

'Cold enough to freeze the balls off a brass monkey' refers to cannonballs freezing on board ship

IN the late nineteenth century, ships' cannonballs were said to be stacked on a brass rack or 'monkey', and in cold weather, the brass would contract and eject the cannonballs. Although the explanation transforms the phrase into the height of respectability, there is not a shred of evidence to tie the tale with the phrase.

The *Oxford Dictionary of Phrase and Fable* says that the term 'monkey' is not otherwise recorded 'in this sense', and adds that 'the rate of contraction of brass in cold temperatures is unlikely to be sufficient to cause the reputed effect.'

In *The Real McCoy*, Peter Chadington reveals that the earliest record of the saying dates back to 1929, which is 'well passed the age of sail'. Furthermore, he points out that the earliest written form is 'cold enough to freeze the tail off a brass monkey'. Interestingly, Chadington quotes a similar saying from Herman Melville's 1847 work *Omoo: A Narrative of Adventures in the South Seas*, which includes the revelation 'it was 'ot [hot] enough to melt the nose h'off a brass monkey.' *Phrase and Fable* suggests that 'the phrase is simply a ribald allusion to the fact that metal figures will become very cold to the touch in cold weather.' The saying remains rude, but you can now substitute the word 'tail' for the naughty noun, since there is sound etymological basis for it being a valid variant.

Chapter 16

SUSPECT SAINTS

St George, the patron saint of England, was English

It's not certain that St George existed. Henry Summerson's entry in the *Oxford Dictionary of National Biography* reveals that St George's 'historicity cannot be established with certainty'. The *Encyclopaedia Britannica* adds that 'nothing of George's life or deeds can be established.' Despite this, or possibly due to it, the almost wholly legendary image of St George survives, albeit as a mystical figure.

The Oxford Dictionary of Saints suggests that 'it is likely but not certain that he was a soldier.' Summerson makes reference to a fourth-century inscription at Shaqqa in the Hauran, (modern-day Syria) which commemorates 'the holy and triumphant martyrs, George and the saints who [suffered martyrdom] with him'. He also suggests that George was probably a Christian who was persecuted by Emperor Diocletian in 303.

George became known in England during the seventh or eighth century. In *Aelfric's Lives of the Saints*, Anglo-Saxon writer Aelfric claimed to have the true history of the warrior saint – although this was just a pared down version of the story doing the rounds in the Mediterranean. Aelfric describes George as a 'rich noble under the cruel Emperor . . . in the province Cappadocia'. He regales us with tales of the pious George surviving poison, being bound on a wheel and being cooked in boiling lead before being finally beheaded by the wicked Emperor. His persecutor came off no better, however, since on his way home he 'was suddenly slain by fire from heaven . . . and he went to hell before he reached his house.'

Defying death so many times (right up until the beheading), hugely raised George's standing in the eastern Mediterranean. Europeans found these feats a bit extravagant and, as Summerson explains, the Roman Church declared that George's deeds, laudable though they were, were known 'only to God'.

George was also the 'bridegroom of Christ'. In *St George*, Dr Samantha Riches explains that the tradition stems from the fifth-century 'Coptic Christian sects of North-east Africa'. She reveals that it 'seems to identify a chaste same-sex marriage between the saints and the divinity as an equivalent of the "mystic marriage" with Christ claimed by St Katherine of Alexandria and some other saintly women.' Riches adds that 'initial research into the topos [literary convention] has suggested that St George may have some claim to be considered as an icon of homosexual love.'

During the thirteenth century, chronicler Jacob de Voragine writing in *Legenda Aurea* (*Golden Legend*) tells how George rescues the daughter of a Libyan king. He 'slew the dragon and smote off his head' but only on condition that everyone got baptized straight afterwards. The fact that dragons are mythical beasts rather casts doubt on the accuracy of this tale.

George became England's patron saint in the early fourteenth century when King Edward III, as *Britannica* explains, 'made him the patron of the newly founded Order of the Garter'. In the fifteenth century, relics of the warrior saint became popular. Summerson reveals that 'a small Augustinian priory in the East Riding of Yorkshire . . . claimed to have an arm'. The Guild Chapel in Norwich Cathedral, Norfolk had another. Not forgetting, of course, the one held at the Saint's Chapel, Windsor in Berkshire.

Well known for being the patron saint of England, St George is, according to Fernando and Gioia Lanzi in *Saints and Their Symbols*, also the patron saint of Boy Scouts, the plague and syphilis. St George is indeed a many faceted figure, but one thing is certain, he was in no respect an Englishman.

St Patrick, the patron saint of Ireland, was Irish

ST PATRICK, who lived in the fifth century, was British. In his spiritual autobiography *[Confession]*, he tells us he was 'of the settlement [vicus] of Bannavem Taburniae'. Bannavem is the place name and Taburniae probably means of the Taburnia tribe. Claire Stancliffe's entry in the *Oxford Dictionary of National Biography* suggests that Patrick's 'villa could well have been in south-west Britain, or perhaps somewhere not too far from the coast between Chester and the Solway Firth.' *Encyclopaedia Britannica* agrees that Patrick was from 'Britain of a Romanized family', while the *Catholic Encyclopedia* proposes that he may have been Scottish, coming from 'Kilpatrick, near Dumbarton'.

St Patrick explains that when he was 'about sixteen years of age' he was 'taken into captivity in Ireland with many thousands of people'. The *Catholic Encyclopedia* claims that 'Irish raiders from the villa of his father, Calpurnius, a deacon and minor local official' carried him into slavery in Ireland, where he spent 'six bleak years . . . as a herdsman [and] he turned with fervour to his faith'. Stancliffe suggests he probably ended up 'on a farm near Killala Bay, in County Mayo'.

Patrick took his chance to escape home by ship. 'After a few years I was again in Britain with my parents [kinsfolk], and they welcomed me as a son, and asked me, in faith, that after the great tribulations I had endured I should not go any where else away from them.' However, he heard a voice call him back to Ireland: 'We beg you, holy youth, that you shall come and shall walk again among us.' He duly answered his calling, and went on to convert almost the whole of Ireland to Christianity.

As well as being the patron saint of Ireland, St Patrick is also reported to have freed Ireland from snakes. *The Concise Oxford Dictionary of the Christian Church* relates that 'he stood on a hill . . . and used a staff to herd the slithering creatures into the sea, banishing them for eternity.' The volume also confirms that 'there are no snakes in Ireland' to this day, but then admits that 'there never were'. *The Biology, Husbandry and Health Care of Reptiles* by Dr Lowell Ackerman reveals that all the snakes in Europe 'were destroyed during the last Great Ice Age, and were unable to repopulate before Ireland became separated from the rest of Europe'.

St Catherine of Alexandria, the patron saint of wheelwrights, was martyred on a spiked wheel

I once asked my mother why the Catherine wheel was so named and was informed it was because St Catherine of Alexandria had been martyred that way. From then on, I imagined St Catherine had been executed by being strapped to a giant firework: a painful but satisfyingly spectacular way to meet one's maker.

St Catherine was reputed to have lived in the fourth century. A popular saint, *Encyclopaedia Britannica* tells how Joan of Arc 'claimed that Catherine's was among the heavenly voices that spoke to her'. However, in *The Oxford Dictionary of Saints*, David Hugh Farmer reveals that there 'is no ancient cult of this saint, no mention in early Martyrologies, no early works of art'. *Britannica* points out that Catherine 'is not mentioned before the ninth century, and her historicity is doubtful'. The *Catholic Encyclopedia* cites eighteenth-century Benedictine Dom Deforis suggesting that many of the stories concerning the saint are 'in a great measure false'. *Britannica* adds that 'in 1969, her feast day was removed from the church calendar'. Farmer explains that 'the cult began in the ninth century at Mount Sinai', which is where her body was supposedly transported by angels after her death.

Even the *legendary* St Catherine wasn't martyred on a wheel. Legend tells us that eighteen-year-old Catherine complained to Roman Emperor Maxentius about his Christian persecutions. The emperor attempted to convert Catherine to the Roman style of worship and, according to some versions, attempted to marry her (bigamously). Far from being converted to Roman worship, Catherine converted some of Maxentius's scholars to Christianity including, it is said, the Empress. For this, Catherine was condemned to die on a spiked wheel, which Maxentius designed specifically for the occasion. *The Chemistry of Fireworks* by Michael Russell confirms that this torture implement prompted 'the evolution of the firework known as "St Catherine's Wheel"'.

However, as the *Catholic Encyclopedia* explains, 'at her touch, this instrument of torture was miraculously destroyed.' Farmer agrees that 'the machine broke down injuring bystanders' as it exploded apart. Michelangelo's *Last Judgement* in the Sistine Chapel shows an extremely muscular Catherine brandishing a piece of her broken, spiked wheel. (She was originally depicted nude but in 1559, Pope Paul IV contracted Daniele da Volterra, nicknamed 'The Breeches Maker', to furnisher her with a green dress.) However, the forthright teenager was not permitted to live and Farmer explains that 'Catherine was beheaded'.

During the fourteenth century, the Catherine wheel brooch was a popular piece of jewellery. In fact, you can still buy them, complete with murderous-looking spikes. How fetching.

St Laurence, the patron saint of cooks, was martyred on a gridiron

THIRD-CENTURY Deacon of Rome, St Laurence is another saint who wasn't quite as martyred as generally believed. According to the *Concise Oxford Dictionary of the Christian Church*, the story goes that the Prefect of Rome asked Laurence to 'deliver up the riches of the Church'. Far too clever for his own good, Laurence presented the Prefect with a collection of paupers and announced 'These are the treasures of the Church.'

Latin poet Aurelius Prudentius Clemens in his fifth-century poem 'Of the Crowns' records that in response the Prefect 'laid him bound upon the pyre'.

However, Laurence had the last laugh, quipping from his 'gridiron', 'Pray turn my body, on one side / [I am] Already broiled sufficiently' adding 'I am well baked, / And whether better cooked or raw, / Make trial by a taste of me.' For those having trouble following the narrative, Prudentius explains that St Laurence 'said these words in way of jest'.

The *Catholic Encyclopedia* warns that Prudentius's tale is 'founded rather on oral tradition than on written accounts'. The *Oxford Dictionary of Saints* by David Hugh Farmer reveals that 'few details of his life are historical'. The *Encyclopaedia* adds that belief in this manner of death gives 'rise to grave doubts'. The *Concise Oxford Dictionary of the Christian Church* states that 'the story is widely rejected by modern scholars.' Farmer points out that in Rome, at that time, 'the contemporary instrument of capital punishment was the sword.'

On a fascinating final note, as well as being the patron saint of cooks, St Laurence is also the patron saint of comics.

Chapter 17

WRONG RELIGION

There was a female pope named Joan

Twelfth-century Pope Joan is fabled for being, some say, an English pontiff whose female gender was only discovered when she inadvertently gave birth in the street while attempting to mount a horse. Even the *Encyclopaedia Britannica* includes an entry describing her as a 'legendary female pontiff who supposedly reigned, under the title of John VIII, for slightly more than 25 months, from 855 to 858.' The *Catholic Encyclopedia* explains that the story of Pope Joan was believed 'in the fourteenth and fifteenth centuries, [when] this popess was already counted as an historical personage, whose existence no one doubted.' Indeed, 'she had her place among the carved busts which stood in Siena Cathedral.'

The first to document the popess was thirteenth-century Dominican chronicler Jean de Mailly in his work *Chronica Universalis Mettensis.* Describing her career progression, he explained that she 'disguised herself as a man and became, by her character and talents, a curial secretary, then a cardinal and finally pope'. De Mailly informs us that 'one day, while mounting a horse, she gave birth.' Instead of being looked after and given a nice cup of tea, the unfortunate popess was 'bound by the feet to a horse's tail and dragged and stoned by the people for half a league'. They buried her where she died and marked the site with the inscription: '*Petre, Pater Patrum, Papisse Prodito Partum*', which author of *The Myth of Pope Joan* Alain Boureau translates as 'Peter, Father of Fathers, Punish the Parturition [childbearing] of the Popess.'

LA·PAPESSE·☒☒

De Mailly's contemporary, the chronicler Martin of Troppau, named the popess in his work *Chronicon Pontificum et Imperatum* as 'John', who was generally referred to as Joan, 'a woman, who as a girl had been led to Athens dressed in the clothes of a man by a certain lover of hers.' He goes on to explain that after 'she was chosen for pope . . . she became pregnant by her companion . . . and was delivered of a child while in procession from St Peter's to the Lateran, in a narrow lane between the Colosseum and St Clement's church.' Troppau informs us that after her death, the unfortunate Joan was not 'placed on the list of the holy pontiffs, both because of her female sex and on account of the foulness of the matter.'

By the fifteenth century, it was claimed that the marble chair used for enthroning the new pope, an ancient bath-stool complete with hole in the seat, was employed to ensure that he *was* a he. But in truth the ancient seat was in use long before the supposed reign of Pope Joan.

As to the question of whether Pope Joan ever existed, Boureau states 'certainly not'. In the *Oxford Dictionary of Popes,* church historian J. N. D. Kelly adds that there is 'no contemporary evidence for a female pope at any of the dates suggested for her reign'. Kelly suggests that the tale's origin is thought to be 'an ancient Roman folk tale.' The *Catholic Encyclopedia* quotes ecclesiastical historian Caesar Baronius, who suggests that the 'effeminate weaknesses of Pope John VIII' may have given rise to the story. It also refers to Photius of Constantinople who 'refers emphatically three times to this pope as "the Manly," as though he would remove from him the stigma of effeminacy.'

Alternatively, the *Catholic Encyclopedia* cites nineteenth-century historical scholar and theologian Johann Joseph Ignaz von Döllinger and his work *Papstfabeln* [Pope Fables], which reveals that in the sixteenth century, near the Colosseum, an ancient statue was discovered depicting a figure with a child. This was generally considered by the populace to represent a popess. In the same street, there was an inscription that began *Pap. pater partum*, which ties in with De Mailly's tale. This inscription could possibly have been construed as *Female father of fathers*. The tale of the popess could have arisen to explain the mysterious statue and nearby inscription.

Pope Benedict IX was installed at the age of twelve

ELEVENTH-CENTURY Pope Benedict IX deserves his notoriety, but not for the reason commonly claimed. In *The Oxford Dictionary of Popes,* J. N. D. Kelly explains that Pope Benedict 'was not, as later gossip alleged, a lad of ten or twelve, but was probably in his late twenties'. The *Catholic Encyclopedia* concludes that he was 'about twenty'. The myth grew up early along with the youthful Benedict. The slipshod, eleventh-century Benedictine chronicler Radulfus Glaber claims in his *History of the Christian Church* (Volume IV) that 'a boy of only ten or twelve years of age ascended the papal throne under the name of Benedict IX.' Perhaps Glaber, who was around fifty at the time of Benedict IX's installation in 1032, was of the opinion that all young people in positions of responsibility looked younger than they were.

Benedict IX may not have been the youngest pope, but he *was* pope three times and he also holds the dubious honour of being the only pope to have sold his papacy. The story began when Benedict's uncle, Pope John XIX, died in 1032 and Benedict's father, Alberic III (head of the ruling Tusculani family) 'bribed the electorate and had his son . . . elected and enthroned, with the style Benedict IX'. Benedict's behaviour as Pope doesn't appear to have justified his papal candidacy,

since Kelly describes his personal life, even allowing for exaggerated reports, as 'scandalously violent and dissolute'. The *Catholic Encyclopedia* admits that Benedict was 'a disgrace to the Chair of Peter', particularly after his second reign, when he 'made out a deed of abdication in favour of his godfather John Gratian' who was elected and styled himself Pope Gregory VI'.

It has been suggested that Pope Benedict IX sold his papacy because nobody liked him, or possibly because he wanted to get married, but there was also the small matter of 'a huge sum of money' which his successor 'had to raise and hand over to him'. The *Catholic Encyclopedia* then describes Benedict as 'repenting of his bargain' and attempting to depose Pope Gregory VI. The upshot was that a new pope, Clement II, was installed in 1046. *Encyclopaedia Britannica* explains that after Pope Clement's death a year later, 'Benedict reappeared in Rome and installed himself' as pope once again, making the hat trick. In 1048, however, Benedict was driven from Rome and replaced with Pope Damasus II.

The title for youngest pope goes to tenth-century Pope John XII, who was installed in 955 at the age of eighteen. Benedict IX, however, retains the title for being the most mercenary pope in papal history.

The Star of David is an ancient Hebrew symbol

THE Star of David, also known as the Shield of David or the *magen* David, is a six-pointed star consisting of two superimposed equilateral triangles. Its origin is unknown and its universal representation of Judaism only occurred in the nineteenth century. The *Macmillan Encyclopedia* states that it was 'widely used from antiquity as an ornament or magical sign', while the *Encyclopedia of World Religions* explains that the symbol has 'no biblical or Talmudic [pertaining to traditional Jewish Law] authority'.

The Jewish Encyclopedia confirms that 'the shield of David is not mentioned in rabbinical literature,' adding that the symbol 'may have been employed originally also as an architectural ornament on synagogues, as it is, for example, on the cathedrals of Brandenburg and Stendal, and on the Marktkirche cathedral at Hanover'. In *The Myth and Reality of Judaism,* Rabbi Simon Glustrom explains that although 'most synagogues display the Star of David . . . as an art form either within the sanctuary or the exterior of the building . . . the symbol does not contain any special religious significance. It serves only to give a Jewish identification to the building.'

Glustrom suggests that the symbol was first used in connection with Judaism in 1354, when King Charles IV 'permitted the Jewish community of Prague to bear its own flag [bearing the star] later called in documents "King David's Flag"'. The star was chosen as the symbol since it was alleged that King David bore it on his shield. The *Macmillan Encyclopedia* adds that in the seventeenth century it was generally regarded as a Jewish symbol, and the *Encyclopedia of World Religions* reveals it was 'almost universally adopted by Jews in the nineteenth century as an emblem of Judaism'. Glustrom confirms that the Zionist movement adopted the symbol in 1948 'as the official emblem on the flag of Israel'.

The English Church burnt millions of women as witches

THE 'Burning Times' are often referred to in popular fiction. It is sometimes claimed that the English Church burnt five million women at the stake (as suggested in *The Da Vinci Code*). Yet Nigel Cawthorne reveals in

The Strange Laws of Old England that 'the Church in England was traditionally lenient on witches.' According to Cawthorne, in 1371, a man arrested for possessing the head of a corpse and a spell book was released 'after promising never to perform magic rites again'. In 1467, William Byng, after being convicted of using a crystal ball to locate thieves, was sentenced to appear in public with a scroll attached to his head, which read: *'Ecce sortilegus'* ['Behold the fortune teller'].

In the mid sixteenth century, witchcraft became a statutory crime, which meant that the state rather than the clergy tried the accused. Brian P. Levack, history professor and editor of *Witchcraft in Scotland,* reveals that 'the number of English executions did not exceed 1,000 and may have been as low as 500.' *Encyclopaedia Britannica* puts 'perhaps 230 or more' of the English executions down to two self-appointed 'witch-finders', namely Matthew Hopkins and John Stearne, who worked in East Anglia between 1645 and 1646. For a fee, they would identify witches. A few of their victims were Anglican clergymen. In 1649, a similar service was provided in Newcastle-upon-Tyne by a Scottish witch-finder (later himself hanged for fraud, according to Ralph Gardiner's 1655 pamphlet *England's Grievance Discovered*), who dispatched fourteen witches and one wizard at twenty shillings per head.

Contrary to common opinion, the condemned were not burnt at the stake. In *Crime and Mentalities in Early Modern England,* Malcolm Gaskill states that 'the statutory punishment was hanging'. One such example is recorded in William Knipe's 1867 work *Criminal Chronology of York Castle.* Thirty-two-year-old Isabella Billington was tried, along with her husband, at York Special Assizes and hanged for witchcraft after 'crucifying her mother at Pocklington, on the 5th day of January, 1649, and offering a calf and a cock for a burnt sacrifice.' After her demise, Isabella's remains were burnt, just for good measure. (Possibly no smoke without fire, there.)

Burning at the stake was reserved solely for witchcraft resulting in the murder of a husband, priest, master or mistress; a crime known as petty treason. Even then the condemned was generally strangled by a cord attached to the neck before the flames took hold. I could only find five documented cases of witch-burning in England. The best known is Margery Jourdemayne at Smithfield in 1441, for high 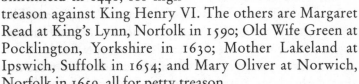 treason against King Henry VI. The others are Margaret Read at King's Lynn, Norfolk in 1590; Old Wife Green at Pocklington, Yorkshire in 1630; Mother Lakeland at Ipswich, Suffolk in 1654; and Mary Oliver at Norwich, Norfolk in 1659, all for petty treason.

The misapprehension that witches were burnt in England appears to date back several centuries. Gaskill cites the 1702 work *The New State of England*, which claimed that 'Burning alive is a Punishment the Law inflicts upon Witches.'

Levack confirms that 'English witches were hanged like other felons' whereas 'Scottish witches were burnt at the stake, a penalty reserved mainly for heretics.'

Scottish executions were a different matter. Levack states that they 'probably stand somewhere between 1,000 and 1,500', which was mainly due to King James I (or James VI as he was in Scotland). The 1591 tract *Newes from Scotland* reveals that, under torture, Agnis Tompson confessed to planning to smear black toad venom onto 'any part or piece of foul linen cloth that had appertained to the King's Majesty' [his undies] with the intent to bewitch him 'to death' by means of imparting the sensation that he was 'lying upon sharp thorns and ends of needles'. In his 1597 witch-hunters' handbook *Daemonologie*, King James stated that there was a 'fearful abounding ... of these detestable slaves of the Devil, the witches or enchanters'.

Certain areas of Europe also advocated burning of witches. In *A Dictionary of World Mythology*, Arthur Cotterell reveals that at the end of the sixteenth century, near the ancient German city of Trier, 'three hundred and sixty-eight witches were burnt, leaving two villages with only one female inhabitant each.'

England, by contrast, appears to have retained its leniency into the seventeenth century. Cawthorne records the case of Jane Wellman of Gloucestershire, who was tried by Mr Justice Powell on charges of being able to fly. Powell questioned the defendant as to whether she could fly. To the consternation of the court, the accused confirmed that she could, to which Powell replied, 'Then you may ... there is no law against flying.'

ACKNOWLEDGEMENTS

THANK YOU to Andy Barham and Margaret Crawley for proofreading the typescript and to Martyn Brinton for mending my computer after it got zapped by a power surge. Thank you to Rupert Willis who furnished me with a surge protector so it wouldn't get zapped again, to Simon Blackman for all the chocolate trifles, and to Helen Cumberbatch for her sensitive copy-editing skills. And last, but not least, thank you to my Kings and Queens of England tea towel, without which I would have been in a right muddle. And frequently was.

Select
Bibliography

Boller, Paul F., *They Never Said It: A Book of Fake Quotes, Misquotes and Misleading Attributions* (OUP, 1990)

Briggs, Asa (ed.), *Who's Who in the Twentieth Century* (OUP, 1999)

Cannon, John (ed.), *The Oxford Companion to British History* (OUP, 2003)

Chadington, Peter, *The Real McCoy: A Dictionary of Peculiar English* (Icon, 2005)

Dear, I. C. B., and Foot, M. R. D. (eds.), *The Oxford Companion to World War II* (OUP, 2001)

Farmer, David Hugh, *The Oxford Dictionary of Saints* (OUP, 2004)

Gambles, R., *Breaking Butterflies: A Study of Historical Anecdotes* (Vanguard Press, 2006)

Hart, James, D., and Leininger, Rev. Phillip W., *The Oxford Companion to American Literature* (OUP, 2002)

Heilbron, J. L. (ed.), *The Oxford Companion to the History of Modern Science* (OUP, 2003)

Select Bibliography

HOLMES, RICHARD (ed.), *The Oxford Companion to Military History* (OUP, 2004)

Hutchinson Encyclopedia (Helicon, 2005)

KELLY, J. N. D., and WALSH, MICHAEL, *The Oxford Dictionary of Popes* (OUP, 2006)

KNOWLES, ELIZABETH (ed.), *The Oxford Dictionary of Quotations* (OUP, 2005)

KNOWLES, ELIZABETH (ed.), *Oxford Dictionary of Phrase and Fable* (OUP, 2006)

LIVINGSTONE, E. A. (ed.), *The Concise Oxford Dictionary of the Christian Church* (OUP, 2006)

The Macmillan Encyclopedia (Market House, 2003)

Oxford Dictionary of National Biography (OUP, 2004)

The Oxford Essential Dictionary of the US Military (OUP, 2001)

The Penguin Biographical Dictionary of Women (Penguin, 1998)

Philip's World Encyclopedia (Octopus, 2003)

RAYNER, ED, and STAPLEY, RON, *Debunking History: 152 Popular Myths Exploded* (Sutton, 2002)

SIMPSON, JACQUELINE and ROUD, STEVE, *A Dictionary of English Folklore* (OUP, 2000)

UGLOW, JENNIFER, and HINTON, FRANCES (eds), *Dictionary of Women's Biography* (Macmillan, 1998)

USEFUL WEBSITES

www.bartleby.com
[searchable quotations site]

www.britannica.com
[Encyclopaedia Britannica]

www.eyewitnesstohistory.com
[Eyewitness accounts of Historical Events}

www.fordham.edu/halsall/sbook1.html
[Medieval Sourcebook]

www.books.google.com
[Google Book Search]

www.newadvent.org
[The Catholic Encyclopedia]

www.oed.com
[Oxford English Dictionary]

www.ota.ahds.ac.uk
[Oxford Text Archive]

www.oxfordreference.com/views/GLOBAL.html
[Oxford Reference Online]

www.promo.net/pg
[Project Gutenberg – electronic books and texts]

www.xreferplus.com/info.jsp
[Credo Reference]

and **www.pedantsrevolt.co.uk**